PEBBLE MOSAICS

The art of
PEBBLE
MOSAICS

Creative designs and techniques for paths and patios

MAGGY HOWARTH

SEARCH PRESS

Acknowledgements

The author would like to express her grateful thanks to: The Winston Churchill Memorial Trust, which gave her the opportunity to track down the pebble mosaics of Spain and Portugal with the help of one of its marvellous Fellowships in 1987. Escuela Taller Carmen de los Martires, in Granada, and Escola de Calceteiros in Lisbon, especially the teacher Fernando Batista, and José Tudella of Lisbon City Council.
Glynn Douglas, Glen Armstrong and John Naylor: a triumvirate of expert advisers who willingly collaborated on the technical aspects of making pebble mosaics to be found in the chapter 'Making Pebble Mosaics *in Situ*'.
Joan Wood, David Hogg and Paul Barnes, for rallying to her cry for help with the drawings.
Mark Currie, her workshop assistant, for his endless tolerance and practical assistance.
Boris Howarth for his collaboration and support at every stage in the creation of this book.

All the photographs are by Maggy Howarth and Boris Howarth except for those which are reproduced by permission of the following agencies and photographers: Calvin Cairns page 11; Robert Harding Picture Library pages 8-9; David Herrod page 94 (top); Peter Hayden page 10; Lancashire Evening Post page 55 (bottom); Nick Lockett page 67 (bottom left); Eduardo Néry page 21; Phil Sayer (by permission of the Crafts Council of Great Britain) page 71 (bottom left); Christian Smith page 22; Alistair Snow pages 31 (bottom left), 71 (top); Norman Tozer page 17. Drawings are by Paul Barnes pages 23, 24, 39, 42 (bottom left and centre), 45; Mark Currie page 70 (bottom left); David Hogg pages 40, 41, 48 (bottom), 49, 58; George Howarth page 78; Joan Wood pages 59, 60, 62 (top), 63. All other drawings are by the author.

Note

The author is always keen to hear of interesting examples of pebble mosaic throughout the world; there is still much to be discovered. If readers come across anything of interest, please contact Maggy Howarth, Hilltop, Wennington, Lancaster LA2 8NY, England.

Page 2 *A sun mosaic in the author's cottage garden.*

Front cover *Circular Capricorn mosaic in a private garden, photographed by Search Press Studios.*

Opposite *A mosaic by the author in a shopping centre at Swindon, Wiltshire. The bird design incorporates carved panels depicting themes from local history.*

First published in Great Britain 1994
Search Press Limited, Wellwood, North Farm Road, Tunbridge Wells, Kent TN2 3DR
in association with David Bateman Ltd, 32-34 View Road, Glenfield, Auckland 10, New Zealand.

Reprinted 1996, 1997

ISBN 0 85532 767 7

If you have difficulty in obtaining any of the materials or equipment mentioned in this book, then please write for further information to the Publishers, Search Press Ltd., Wellwood, North Farm Road, Tunbridge Wells, Kent TN2 3DR.

Designed by Errol McLeary
Printed in Hong Kong by Colorcraft Ltd

CONTENTS

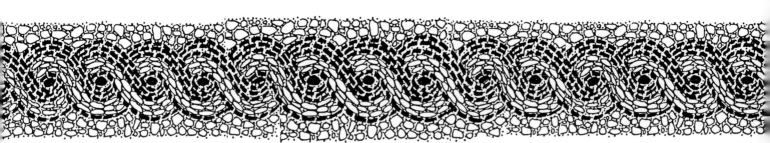

FOREWORD

Everyone loves pebbles! Pick up a pebble from a beach or river bed and feel the smoothness of its contours, enjoy the range of its colours, and compare the infinite variety of shapes formed by the great forces of wind and water in a continuous action of grinding and rolling. From the child collecting a hoard of pebble treasures, to the philosopher considering the unending process of nature, how can anyone resist their fascination?

Not long ago, before the invention of heavy machinery, pebbles were considered a valuable resource: an easy-to-use raw material for making floors in buildings and for surfacing pavements and roads. Where they were not available, enormous labour was required to quarry, to cut and to crush stone for these purposes. So it is not surprising to find that pebbles were in regular use as a paving surface in areas where they naturally occurred. They were hard-wearing, and their many shapes and colours provided the opportunity for a variety of decorative effects — for the making of mosaics.

Pebble mosaics have been used to surface floors and paths, and occasionally walls too. The true pebble mosaic is formed from water-worn pebbles packed to a level, and the gaps between them filled with finer material, such as sand. These pebbles occur naturally on shingle banks, beaches or river banks. Other types of mosaic usually involve the *cutting* of stone or glass and ceramic pieces which are then fitted together. Larger stones are often known as cobbles and they may include rough material collected from fields.

The ancient Greeks were among the first to make mosaic floors from pebbles; but in fact they have been made wherever there is a good supply. They were created centuries ago in China, produced with great skill by the Arab civilization of Spain, and employed in the gardens of Renaissance Italy and on the streets of northern Europe, and the same techniques were taken across the Atlantic to the Americas.

The particular beauty of pebble mosaic is in the texture it gives to a surface. A pebble mosaic is comfortable to walk on and has excellent non-slip qualities, with the added interest of the pebbles and the different patterns which can be made. With wear and age, pebbles become attractively polished on the top.

My involvement in pebble mosaic started from an interest in gardens. While developing our rural garden on a hilltop in Lancashire, I redesigned a cottage garden area in front of the house and decided to try my hand at cobbling. In this north-western corner of England, small patches of fine cobblework

can still be seen in nearby towns and villages, adding a quiet charm to the surroundings, and I set out to follow this tradition. Whilst not wishing to walk on pebbles all the time, I wanted to make a small decorative area for my own pleasure, and as a welcome for visitors.

This beginning led to more experiments. The pebble mosaics seemed to strike a chord with many visitors. Those who did not appreciate them as art were happy to see the results of laborious craftsmanship.

As an artist, it was not long before I realised the possibilities of the medium, not only as a garden ornament but as a way of making decorative pavements which might help to alleviate some of the boredom of modern townscapes. These are so often carpeted with the uniformly smooth, convenient and oh-so-dull hard surfaces which we have come to accept.

My own work has led to the devising of a pre-cast technique for creating commissions away from site. It is a practical solution to the problem of co-ordinating with building contractors working all over the country, and allowing large works to be assembled in their final location in a few days. However, making pebble mosaic in the traditional *in situ* fashion has much to recommend it, and the technique may be grasped easily by someone attempting it for the first time. It is direct, spontaneous and rewarding.

In this book, I want to share with the reader my own enthusiasm for pebble mosaic. We will look at several kinds, from the humble utilitarian pavement to the sophisticated decorative floors of some great houses and gardens, and including some other forms of mosaic which are closely related.

For those of you who would like to make use of your precious hoard of holiday pebbles or devise a small piece for your own doorstep or patio, the instructions for making mosaic are carefully explained. If, made ambitious by your success, you want to tackle more complex work, there are directions for that, too. In the illustrations of historical and modern mosaics and the original designs, you will find a great variety of ideas from which to develop your own themes. Feel free to use any of my designs for your own private work: I wish you every success. (For commercial reproduction see note on copyright on page 4.)

In the public sphere, our attitude towards the urban environment is changing: people increasingly feel the need for more human interest and variety, attractive textures and decoration. I hope this book will encourage landscape architects and garden designers to incorporate pebblework into their schemes. The individuality and character of pebbles in well-designed and properly made mosaic pavements can add a touch of magic to an otherwise undistinguished environment.

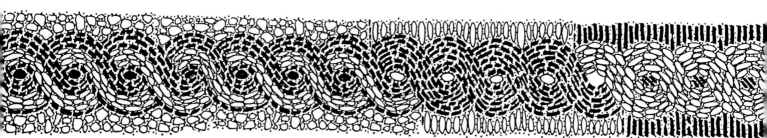

PEBBLE MOSAIC: The Tradition

The pebble mosaic tradition was born thousands of years ago, out of domestic necessity. It is a part of the long, and largely unrecorded, history of the common floor. Excavations in Spain and along the Mediterranean have revealed the attempts of early peoples to surface the ground on which they built their dwellings. These first attempts were simply crust-forming exercises. Pounded clay was sealed with lime to form a hard surface which was suitable for sweeping, without making clouds of dust. Unfortunately it needed frequent repair, and was often renewed, layer upon layer.

Pliny, the chronicler of ancient Rome, refers to floors which were surfaced with lime and crushed pottery. Pressing small elements into the clay as the floor was constructed gave it reinforcement; and, at the same time, was a way of adding decoration. Where pebbles were near to hand, they offered a similar way of reinforcing and decorating the floor — a much more attractive surface than beaten earth.

The earliest recorded pebble mosaic floor is found at Gordium in Asia Minor, and dates from the eighth century BC. It is composed of simple chequerboard patterns. Examples from Spain of a similar date suggest that pebble mosaic flooring, along with the other types of semi-surfaced beaten earth floors, was probably in widespread use in the Mediterranean region from the eighth century BC onwards.

Pebble mosaics of ancient Greece

By the end of the fourth century BC, pebble mosaics of amazing quality were being produced in Greece. Especially fine are those excavated in 1955–63 in Pella, in northern Greece, capital of Macedonia and birthplace of Alexander the Great. Here the use of the pebbled surface is far removed from a mere domestic expedient: the technique has been developed and refined, and the resulting surface has become a medium for the artist.

The designs, which include hunting scenes and the god Dionysus riding on a panther, are closely related in style to the painting and ceramic decoration of the period. The human figure has been studied and drawn to express an ideal of beauty and strength. In the hunting scenes the men are poised in the act of a noble contest with their prey: a pursuit worthy of gods and the highest human endeavour. With a very limited colour range and using quite small pebbles, these mosaics present a very sophisticated artistic concept.

Below *The 'Lion Hunt' mosaic at Pella in Macedonia, Greece, dates from the fourth or early third century* BC. *The palace floors at Pella are some of the finest pebble mosaics ever made. The figures are drawn with studied expression and refinement. The style owes a great deal to the ceramic decoration of the period, and the execution is impeccably disciplined and finely detailed.*

Right *The technique employed in the Pella pebble mosaics is worth a close look. Strips of lead form the outline of the figures and are used to contain the pebbles, as well as precisely defining the contours and main lines. The pebbles are selected for uniformity of size in a limited number of colours. This method made possible the concept of sophisticated floors using pebbles.*

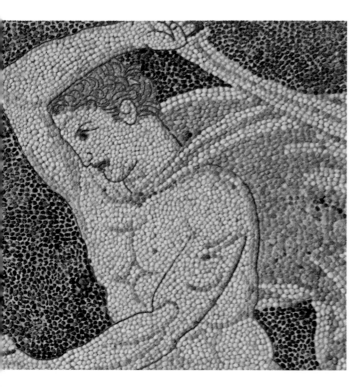

Refreshments for the heart

Chinese civilization began to develop around 3000 BC. Apart from the commercial traffic on the Silk Road, there was little contact with the West until the eighteenth century, but the concept and technology of pebble mosaics was in existence there long before. It was one of the hard surfacing techniques which was used in the gardens of ancient China.

The art of garden-making was established in China before the dawn of the Christian era. Its roots lay in the philosophies of Taoism and Buddhism. An essential element of both these religions is a deep contemplation of nature. The Chinese garden offered a microcosm of the wider landscapes of the natural world. Everything in a Chinese garden has a symbolic value and its forms must strike a balance between *yin* (the dark and feminine) and *yang* (the bright and masculine). Rocks, mountains and water, height, contour, shade and sunshine, were all elements in this process.

This old tradition can still be seen in some private gardens of the Suzhou Province in China. In the Sung Dynasty (960–1229), the Chinese capital was established at Hangchow, and Suzhou became an important stronghold. It was an area of great wealth and the cultural centre of China. Many local government officers retired here to build houses and develop gardens. There were plentiful supplies of water and Lake Tai was the source of rocks, eroded into complex forms, which were a much sought-after form of garden decoration.

Garden construction reached a peak during the sixteenth, seventeenth and eighteenth centuries, when aristocrats and officials competed with each other in garden design. In the Suzhou garden style, pebble mosaic pavements were an important element in the overall scheme, and the geometric patterns of the pavements related to those of the openwork stone 'windows' and internal lattice screens of the buildings and garden pavilions. These pebbles were more than a practical garden surface; they too had a place in the philosophical order of things, where rock in all its forms served as a spiritual springboard for the imagination. The discipline of the rich decorative 'carpets' of pebbles contrasted with carved architectural forms, and with the huge and tortured limestone rocks carefully arranged at the water's edge and in significant locations.

Another aspect of Chinese pebble mosaic art can be seen in the Imperial Palace in Beijing. Tucked away in the back yard are to be found some remarkable pebble pictures: images of a crane, a cat, a warrior, even a man on a bicycle. Part of a restoration of historic work, they include obviously modern additions, but there is no doubt about their artistry. These mosaics are remarkable for their inspired use of available materials to create the images. Shards of ceramic roof tile are particularly well used to make flower patterns and peacock-feather effects, and carved stone details are sometimes incorporated.

Amongst other pebble pictures occasionally to be found in Chinese gardens are pleasing floral designs, where the shapes of petals are improvised with long thin pebbles, and the stems with curved tile shards. It is rare indeed to see pebble mosaic made with such freedom and spontaneity. They form a marked contrast to the rigidly geometric patterned 'carpets' of the surrounding pavements.

Roman mosaics

As far as is known, pebble mosaic techniques were not used at all in ancient Rome, but Roman designs, using cut stones, deserve examination. Many colours of stone were used, and the resulting cubes, called tesserae, were set in a mortar of lime and pounded brick, mixed with water. Sometimes volcanic ash ('Pozzolana') was used, a material which has setting qualities akin to modern Portland cement. The design was scratched into the mortar, and when the tesserae had been laid, the crevices were grouted with a mix-

Right *The Dr Sun Yat-Sen Garden in Vancouver, Canada, was created for Expo '86. The only full-scale traditional classical Chinese garden outside China, it was built by a team of fifty-two Chinese craftsmen from Suzhou. The pebble technique is both interesting and very practical for the construction of repetitive geometric patterns. The ground is hammered flat, then covered with a 5mm (2in) layer of sifted earth in which the patterns are laid. First, the geometric shapes are delineated by strips of cut slate, and then the carefully selected pebbles, of four different colours, are laid into each section in varying directions.*

Left *One of the remarkable pebble pictures found in the 'back yard' of the Imperial Palace in Beijing, this is an example of a decorative and linear style of pebble mosaic design. The Chinese cat is 'drawn' with an outline of grooved stone and the ears, face and feet are carved with expressive detail. The body of the cat is filled in with just a few pebbles to suggest the markings of a tabby cat's fur.*

ture of lime and pounded white marble. This technical sophistication indicates an ideal of thoroughness, which is attested by the survival of so many Roman mosaics.

There were plenty of slaves to chop the tiny cubes and practise the laborious art of fitting them together. Rich Romans loved to decorate their houses with exuberant realistic imagery and rich geometric pattern. Their artists and craftsmen were masters of design: subdividing floors with interlocking shapes, delineated by borders and sub-borders, often framing scenes from the lives of gods, mortals and animals. These elaborate mosaic floors are found throughout the former Empire, and the acutely observed portraits of people, and realistic studies of birds and animals, teach us a great deal about Roman culture: their physical prowess and military achievement, their love of hunting and luxurious living. Above all, Roman mosaics are a fine source of design inspiration and their patterns can often be adapted to pebble forms.

Moorish Spain

Whilst the Roman villas and palaces were usually decorated with marble tesserae mosaics, the pebble tradition was preserved in Moorish Spain. From the sixth to the fourteenth century, the Arab Kingdom of

The floors of a Roman villa at Conimbriga in Portugal, decorated with tesserae mosaics. The variety of designs in Roman mosaics offers a rich source of ideas for inventive methods of space division, as well as effective border patterns, which can be adapted for pebble mosaic.

Right *Paths in the gardens of the Generalife, in Granada, show a variety of patterns, rosettes, plant forms, scrolls and diamonds, for which simple formwork or stencils would have been used. The Generalife mosaics are usually two colours — just black and white. Two distinct types of stone are used: elongated black pebbles, which are usually arranged in a herringbone pattern, giving a directional thrust to the drawn lines, and more rounded white stones, which form an effective all-over background.*

Andalusia was a centre of culture, art and learning. The medieval cities of Cordoba, Seville and Granada were famous for their achievements in medicine, irrigation, agriculture, philosophy, and mathematics. Andalusia was extremely prosperous; weapons, wrought iron, enamel, jewellery, goldsmith's work, textiles and pottery were manufactured and traded all over the Mediterranean. The University of Cordoba was world famous, and many Christians from Western Europe studied alongside the Muslim students. There were free primary schools for poor

This lovely path from the Generalife gardens of Granada shows the possibilities of designing 'a mano' — drawing directly in the sand with the finger to determine the main lines of the design. It is a technique which allows the maker to respond intuitively to the space; to twist a flower into a corner or to twirl a line around a tree. It is one of the charms of the handmade pavement and, with little extra effort, you can tailor the details to the vagaries of the site.

based on the concept of Paradise on earth; of repose, beauty and refinement of the senses. To those in the heat of the Mediterranean sun, Paradise meant shade, scented plants and cooling water. They developed a brilliant technology, not only in the cultivation of plants, but in the management of water to create fountains, basins, and tiny refreshing canals. Flanking these, and defining the geometry of the garden, were paths, decorated and enlivened with pebble mosaics.

Islam's fundamental prohibition of any representation of the human figure channelled the decorative arts of Islam into explorations of other possibilities. On the one hand, the written word took on an abstract form as calligraphic art; and on the other, mathematics led to the development of complicated interwoven geometric designs. Moorish paths and courtyards abound with complex pattern and intricate texture. The finest examples are to be seen in the gardens of the Alhambra and the Generalife in Granada.

In the Andalusian tradition, there is pattern in plenty, but there is also a variety of delightful, freely drawn flower designs, which contrast pleasantly with the earlier rigorous geometry, and spread their tendrils out into the space in an informal and apparently spontaneous manner.

The tradition of the pebble mosaic pavement persisted after the demise of the Arab Kingdom. Today, most towns and villages in southern Spain boast some decorative pebble pavements, though few are as fine as those of the Alhambra.

children, and even peasants could read and write; whilst in the rest of Europe, kings and nobles were often illiterate.

This civilized community was the target of many Christian Crusades. In their wake, following the gradual fragmentation of Andalusia into smaller kingdoms, Granada finally fell to King Ferdinand V in 1492. So Spain was united under Christendom, and the Moors were vanquished; but Arab art, literature and science had made a deep and lasting impression on Spanish culture, which can still be felt today.

The atmosphere of sophistication and prosperity enabled the art of garden-making to flourish. It was

Pebble mosaics of the Italian Renaissance

The Renaissance, Europe's blooming of artistic and scientific endeavour, and the rediscovery of the culture of Classical Greece and Rome, led to the creation of some remarkable gardens during the period from the fourteenth to the seventeenth centuries. Italian designers often favoured pebble mosaic as an outdoor surface for both pavements and walls. They created terraces, grand flights of steps with balustrades, grottoes, nymphaea, and complex waterworks with cascades, fountains and still pools. Architecture was of prime importance and statuary was everywhere (often collections of antique sculpture). Cypress trees were planted to create shaded cool walks and, with clipped topiary, formed a background to the architecture. The gardens are a magnificent monument to man's domination of nature. They express grandeur, a love of luxury and an exuberant energy.

The pebble mosaic, which had continued for hundreds of years as a humble domestic tradition,

was now re-created in the grand manner as a decorative surface in noble gardens.

Some of the finest work can be seen in Tuscany, where pebble mosaic was used to decorate steps and terraces. It was also used to fine effect in the floors of grottoes, those fashionable garden follies where unwary visitors might be subjected to a drenching from jets of water concealed in niches and statuary. The remarkable craftsmanship is confirmed by the durability of the mosaics in the garden of the Villa Torrigiani, near Lucca, which dates from the mid-seventeenth century. The work is sometimes very finely textured, using tiny pebbles less than 25mm (1in) in diameter. Pebblework on this scale represents a Herculean feat of skill, determination and patience.

Italian influence on Northern Europe

Italian garden designs had a considerable influence on the development of other grand gardens throughout Europe, and their features were often imitated. In the eighteenth and nineteenth centuries, young gentlemen often undertook a Grand Tour of European

Left *Geometrical and floral designs on the paths of the Villa Garzoni gardens in Tuscany, Italy.*

Below *The restored stableyard in Whitehaven Castle, Cumbria. A well-preserved pebble pavement more than 250 years old.*

15

cities, especially those of Italy, as part of their education. They were accompanied by a knowledgeable tutor, and visited villas and palaces to study the art and architecture of the Renaissance, travelling from Granada to Seville, from Rome to Florence. It is not difficult to imagine a young man returning home and longing to re-create, in his own grounds, the glories he had seen. Much that was essentially foreign may have been forgotten, but pebblework was an indigenous craft, albeit humble! All that was needed to raise it to this new level was inspiration and design.

How else can we explain the extraordinary mosaic in Whitehaven Castle, reliably dated pre-1740? It seems to translate the style of Italy into a home-grown 'cobblestone' back yard. Geometric stars and scroll work are combined in truly eccentric English fashion, with a pack of the Earl of Lonsdale's favourite foxhounds galloping around the perimeter.

Compared to Italian mosaic, the execution is crude, but the mosaic's continuing durability attests to the sound technique of the English craftsmen. There are three colours: reddish sandstone, blue-grey

The black and white pebble mosaic at Powerscourt, County Dublin, Eire, is in sharp contrast to the rich green contours of this Irish landscape garden.

igneous stones, and whitish quartz; all available from nearby beach deposits. Another example from the same period is to be found in the stables of Levens Hall in Cumbria, which is well known for its remarkable Dutch topiary garden.

Grand English country house estates, such as Stourhead, had pebble floors in grottoes and nymphaea. There are also extensive mosaics on the nineteenth-century Italianate steps and terraces at Powerscourt in Ireland; part of a long vista from the house to the lake and the landscape beyond. Dated 1875, they show geometric devices of circles, stars and crescents with wide plain borders. However, in the translation from Italy to Ireland, something has been lost! The design is dull, although the situation and intention are magnificent.

European styles also inspired American gardens and, although large pebble designs are not often found, an exciting use of pebble mosaic can be seen in the gardens of Dumbarton Oaks, near Washington D.C. There, pebbles have been used in several places, but especially in a water feature of great originality. Pebbles form the base of a shallow pool which is subdivided into a kind of water parterre with curving walls of stone. It is the creation of Beatrix Farrand, the famous American designer. The concept of the formal stately water garden is interwoven with sen-

suous lines and intriguing texture. The pebbles, though plain, are placed in beautifully radiating lines, complementing the shape of each segment of the pool.

The vernacular tradition

It is hard to imagine what roads and paths were made of before the advent of asphalt and concrete. The Romans, who built fine roads throughout Britain and other outposts of their Empire, used graded layers of stone, surfaced with trimmed stone blocks or cobbles — a sound technique. These magnificent roads were a luxury lost when the Empire fell. Medieval travel became a nightmare of struggling on rutted tracks, knee-deep in mud, or thick with dust. In Britain, for instance, only the construction of the turnpike roads in the eighteenth century made it again possible for wheeled traffic to proceed with ease for any considerable distance.

In great cities, roads were expensively paved with slabs of stone, while the less prosperous towns and

At Dumbarton Oaks, near Washington D.C., Beatrix Farrand used pebble mosaics in several places, including this water garden. Here pebbles in sweeping curves on the base of the pools form a counterpoint to the arabesques of stone and raised planting beds.

villages had to be content with the smaller and less evenly surfaced cobblestone. Properly made, a cobbled street is a thing of great visual character and practical utility. However, rattling over it in a horse-drawn carriage, or tripping over the occasional prominent stone to fall flat on your face into a pot-hole filled with water, must have held less charm for the citizens of yesteryear.

Many of the old cobbles are still there, buried beneath the smooth roll-out surfaces of tarmac and concrete, which were adopted so gratefully when they became available. Motor traffic has increased the tide of change. Nowadays, you are lucky indeed if you come across an area of old cobbling still in daily use. In rural areas, conservative habits have resisted change, and modest patches of plain pebble-work can be found around farm houses and country cottages, around churches and in the farm buildings of country estates; the sort of place where people took a pride in achieving a flat surface and an even texture. Their quiet decorative qualities have proved a saving grace.

The materials used vary from place to place. Most often they are whatever small-scale material happens to be available close at hand. Small rocks, picked from ploughed fields, were frequently used around farmyards where it was essential to form a cheap

17

1

2

3

hard surface which would otherwise be churned to a quagmire by the animals.

For finer work, evenly graded, matched pebbles were picked from rivers, streams and beaches, and hauled to the intended site. Such pieces of fine work represented a considerable investment in labour and were a matter of pride to their owners.

1 *The owner of this eighteenth-century house on Castle Hill, Lancaster, went to the trouble to import selected pebbles from a considerable distance to make this effective chequered forecourt.*

2 *Folk designs, such as this windmill and anchor, feature in Lytham St Annes' seafront park. They were made around 1910 to extend the facilities of the developing resort.*

3 *Here simple patterning is achieved through the directional placing of stones in this plain pebblework path near the estate cottages at Traquair House, in the Borders region of Scotland.*

Below *A smart new public space: Plaza del Campo del Principe, in Granada, a pebble pavement made by the Escuela de Carmen de los Mantires. The design uses traditional motifs within a modern mode of space division. Note the pleasing effect when seats and lamp-posts are 'designed in'.*

Indeed, the finest examples are found where there is a good source of material close to hand. At Lytham St Annes, in Lancashire, England, some surviving pavements can be seen, and may once have extended throughout this eighteenth-century fishing village. At that time, the foreshore was stacked high with the kind of elliptical 'skimmer' pebbles which make the best pavements.

The designs were simple: part of an English visual folk tradition of easily recognizable images — a bonny sailing ship, a windmill, a heart, a crown, an anchor. They were unpretentious and easily recognized, even when made by the most unpractised hand.

Occasionally, this vernacular type of pebblework was taken up by garden owners and applied to a more dignified setting. A recurring motif of red hearts adorns almost every gateway at Pitmedden House in the Grampian region of Scotland. It is the emblem from the family coat of arms, picked out in areas of large split cobbles: an unusual technique which gives an excellent level surface.

Portuguese cut stone

Portugal's ubiquitous mosaic pavements are not strictly pebblework, but are made up of cut stone

blocks. Portugal was influenced by the occupation of both Romans and Moors. They left their mark in many aspects of the culture, not least in a love of decorative floors and pavements. Yet the fierce individualism of this small corner of the Iberian Peninsula produced a new hybrid form. Provided with abundant suitable material (hard calcareous limestone), the Portugese invented their own style of mosaic pavement using small cubes of stone about 50mm (2in) square, fitted tightly together. The technique involves shaping the tiny blocks to precise shapes, enabling sharply defined images to be created. It is a difficult art: the block is held in one hand whilst slivers of the stone are chipped off with the sharp edge of a hammer to form the triangles and hexagons which are required for different styles.

Portuguese designs offer many ideas for pebble work. Often they reflect the proud maritime tradition of this tiny country, whose voyagers were sent out by King Henry the Navigator to explore the world. As well as patterns and decorative geometric motifs and inscriptions, there are ships, fish, sea patterns and dolphins.

Pavements with setts

In north European countries, the use of setts for paving is widespread. Setts are riven blocks of stone, usually granite, which make a very hardwearing surface. Many visitors to the continent remark upon the beautiful radiating 'fans' in the streets and squares, made from this carefully graded material. Creating these patterns involves the use of many different sizes which are specially produced by quarries, each block being further shaped on site, when necessary.

Germany's patterned sett-work uses stone in a variety of colours: red, light grey, dark grey, buff, white, black and deep yellow. The careful geometric designs, executed with great precision, have some affinity with Portuguese techniques, although they are of a more robust and sombre character. Indeed, the scale of the blocks is only a little larger than the Portuguese style, which is remarkable, considering the intractable nature of granite.

A mosaic pavement in the Praca de Republica, Redondo, Portugal. Eduardo Néry is a contemporary artist designing public spaces and using the traditional mosaic technique. A thoroughly twentieth-century artist, he shows great panache in his admirable abstract designs; and yet his work continues the tradition of bold 'optical' effects, such as the wave-patterned pavement of the Rossio in Lisbon which dates (incredibly) from 1848.

Modern pebble mosaics

Except in Spain and Portugal, the art of the decorated pavement has been in decline in recent times. Even in Spain there is a struggle to maintain existing pavements and to keep up the training necessary for the construction of new mosaics. The work was poorly paid and held in low esteem. Under the auspices of the Ayuntamiento, the School of Carmen de los Martires in Granada is responsible for training craftsmen, with the help of EC grants and unemployment programmes. Several new pavements and squares have been made in recent years, and it must be hoped that these sterling efforts to keep the craft tradition alive will be maintained.

However, the Spanish tradition of the pebble mosaic pavement is largely a matter of copying old designs. There is little innovation. Artists shun such mundane means of expression, and craftsmen cling to the security of the tried and tested. A refreshing exception to this rule is the work of Raphael Gimenez of Cordoba, a builder and self-taught draughtsman. He makes pleasant, if derivative, designs in his own decorative style: crisp, unaffected and beautifully executed. He is responsible for mosaics in many private gardens in the affluent suburbs of Cordoba and has carried out important restoration work in public

A fine contemporary pebble mosaic by Raphael Gimenez at the Viana Palace in Cordoba, crisply executed in small pebbles.

spaces, particularly the historic Viana Palace. His work shows the highest standard of craftsmanship.

Similarly in Lisbon, Portugal, efforts are being made by the City Council to train young men to carry on the tradition. Like Spain, Portugal boasts its own modern pavement artist. Eduardo Néry has established an admirable working relationship with several contemporary architects, and has designed vast landscaping schemes with mosaic pavements. He draws on the tradition of bold geometric and optical patterns, which he re-creates with a confident sophisticated knowledge of abstract design, combining this with his own witty style of architectural allusion.

The Portuguese paving technique is also used in Brazil. With its modern abstract designs, it has long passed the stage of being an imported colonial style. The work of Roberto Burle Marx is internationally known, especially the seafront at the Copacabana Beach in Rio de Janeiro.

Pebble mosaic practitioners elsewhere are few and far between, but pebble mosaic has lost none of its appeal and it is to be hoped that artists and craftsmen will continue to develop new and invigorating designs.

PRINCIPLES AND MATERIALS

Let us examine in detail the way in which pebble mosaics should be made. By studying surviving pavements made from cobblestones and pebbles, we can see how strength is gained from their physical construction, without the need for 'glues', such as cement, to hold the stones together. Cement is a modern addition which gives added security, but should never replace proper technique.

The four essential principles are:

- a firm base upon which to bed the pebbles.
- a firm side support all round.
- all stones must be placed vertically, thus presenting their smallest surface to the air.
- all stones must be tightly packed, one against another, so that there can be no movement in any direction.

Shapes of stones for pebble mosaics

Only certain shapes of stones are suitable for making pebble mosaic. When collecting pebbles for mosaic use, a strict selection procedure must be adopted or you will not be able to meet the principles of construction outlined above. All stones should be suffi-

ciently elongated to pack together vertically. If design imperatives and lack of choice lead you to use stones with little depth, they may become detached with the effects of weight, wear and weather.

Pebbles can usually be identified as belonging to one of the following groups:

Longs or skimmers Thin flying saucer shapes which are wonderfully expressive. They give a flow and a direction which can be exploited in the design.

Left *The floor mosaic in the boathouse at Birkenhead Park uses motifs of waterfowl and fish inspired by its lakeside setting. A recent pebble mosaic designed by the author.*

Below *A cross-section of an old pavement.*

Above *This pavement at Lytham St Annes is 150 years old and in perfect condition.*

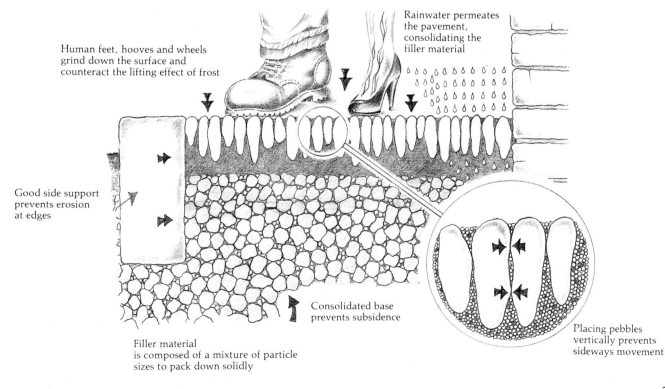

Human feet, hooves and wheels grind down the surface and counteract the lifting effect of frost

Rainwater permeates the pavement, consolidating the filler material

Good side support prevents erosion at edges

Consolidated base prevents subsidence

Filler material is composed of a mixture of particle sizes to pack down solidly

Placing pebbles vertically prevents sideways movement

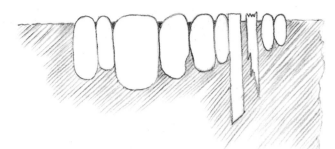

Good and bad shapes of pebbles. Even rounded stones should be sufficiently elongated to pack together vertically. Note that the shape on the extreme right may work loose as the cement mortar shrinks away from the stone.

Cylinders Rounded shapes which make an attractive all-over texture by themselves. They are useful for different patterns and also suggest scaly forms.

Flat-tops Stones with a flat top, often angular, which make a quite different, but equally attractive, overall texture. They can be a larger size than is normally used, making intriguing contrasts with the smaller pebbles.

Quarry stone Selected pieces of broken stone. Some kinds cleave naturally, to give flat angular surfaces which can be fitted together in mosaic-like patterns.

Suitable and unsuitable types of stone	
SUITABLE	UNSUITABLE
Granite (fine-grained)	Mudstones
Slate	Shales
Dolerite	Soft & grainy
Syenite	sandstones
Hard limestone	Marble
Sandstone (fine-grained)	
Quartz	
Flint	
Chert	

Types of stone

Pebbles must be hard so that they will not crush or shatter. If in doubt, test them by hitting them against a rock. Anything which is damaged is obviously not up to the job.

You will find that most fine-grained beach pebble types are suitable for making mosaic. After all, pebbles which have been pounded by the action of sea or river *must* be hard, otherwise they would be sand! However, when collecting, beware of pieces of brick which may look like attractive warm red

Special stones may suggest a whole design, as in this bird, which began with distinctive shapes for the bird's body.

pebbles but will not be frost-hardy. Also avoid very grainy sandstone: it will not wear well, and its coarse surface holds algae which turn the stones green. Some pebbles, such as quartzite and limestone, have holes, cracks and veins which are weak points. These should also be rejected.

Stone colours

Brightly coloured stones are hard to find, and even harder to amass in sufficient quantity to make a pebble mosaic! However, even a small collection of bright coloured stones will be valuable when used for jewel-like details within a background of plainer stones.

The brightest colours of stones are found in igneous rocks: the granites and quartz-bearing formations. They yield reds, pinks, creamy whites, and silvery greys, with the occasional bright red and yellow ochre cherts, as well as brilliant white- and yellow-stained quartz.

The main contrasts of light and dark can be found with pale grey and white limestones, and dark igneous rocks such as dolerite. Sandstones and flints give mid-tones of cream, brown and red.

A selection of pebble types (from left unless specified).

Top row LONGS OR SKIMMERS: dark igneous pebbles, limestone, fine-grained granite.

Left centre (clockwise from top left) FLAT-TOPS: sandstones, fine-grained granites, basalt types.

Right centre CYLINDERS: quartz veined with pink, fine-grained granite, limestone, brown flints.

Centre ANGULAR QUARRY MATERIAL: Italian quartzite (top), black basalt types, coarse-grained red granite, stoneware tiles cut into strips, white quartz.

Below centre TILES AND STONE STRIPS: stoneware tiles cut into strips, ceramic shards, riven slate.

Bottom COLOURED STONES: various granites, hard red sandstone, yellow and white quartz, yellow ochre and red cherts.

The groups are separated by machined slate offcuts and riven slate.

Special stones

A pebble formed of two or more types of stone, which has been worn so that it displays concentric rings, makes an excellent eye for a design with a face or animal head. A good 'eye stone' will give the whole figure character and expression. Look for beaches where two colours of stone are banded: occasionally you will find one. Into the general category of 'specials' must be placed all the unclassifiable, irresistible, individual and mysterious accidents of nature which are found during the collecting process. Sometimes there are enough of them to be worth while collecting for a special purpose. For instance, I have a heap of 'holey' limestones, which I am going to use to make a sheep one day; but they are not really durable, so this will have to be a 'fun' project for a wall panel.

Gravels

Various commercial gravels can be obtained easily from builders' merchants. 'Pea' gravels are the best type to associate with pebbles, since they are natural water-worn materials. I have used them as a surface layer, pressed into wet concrete, for the surround of a pebble mosaic of similar colour.

Gravel is occasionally useful as a filler between flat-surfaced stones (such as tiny slate-fragment figures). Coloured gravels are especially useful when working with children, who can use them to fill in the

'Specials' and non-stone materials (from left). **Top half** *box of tiny pebbles for a special purpose, bone pins used in the ceramic industry, gravels (commercial white feldspar above, flinty 'pea' gravel below), box of coloured glass smalti, box of 'Regulox' and larger-sized grinding material.* **Lower half** *various 'stones of character' which suggest particular uses, a collection of 'eyes', large glass marbles, cores from stone-working quarries, and holed stones.*

awkward gaps which will inevitably occur in this type of work.

Cut stone

To this basic range can be added linear shapes of cut stone, tiles and riven slate. These elements make a sharp contrast with the water-worn pebbles, and add definition to many design motifs, such as the midribs of a leaf, or the coils of a spiral.

A useful by-product of stone-working quarries are the perfectly round 'cores' which are produced during the drilling process. Often they are thrown away, and may be had for the asking. Their machined appearance can sometimes be a useful contrast to the pebbles.

Larger pieces of flat stone can be shaped and carved to insert amongst the pebbles, adding a whole new dimension, and opening up design possibilities for features which are difficult to represent in pebbles alone. They need to be at least 25mm (1in) thick,

Cutting and carving stone

Stone can be cut and carved with a small angle grinder; a most useful and relatively inexpensive tool. The best size is 100mm (4in). It should be fitted with stone-cutting and grinding discs. Use it carefully: it is *essential* to wear goggles to protect the eyes from flying stone particles, and to use vice or pliers for holding small pieces of stone.

If you want to achieve more precise effects than are possible with an angle grinder, you will have to equip yourself with tungsten-tipped stone-carving chisels from specialized masonry suppliers, and learn the difficult art of stone carving.

preferably more, for bedding into the mosaic. Suitable offcuts can often be purchased cheaply from quarries or stone masons.

Other materials

Some man-made materials associate well with natural pebbles and are useful for contrasts in pattern and colour.

By-products of the ceramic industry are worth investigating: kiln furniture, 'bone pins' and ceramic 'shards' are useful. Ceramic materials should be fired to stoneware temperatures, or they will crack up in frost. Stoneware floor tiles in earth colours — grey-blue, terracotta, cream and black — are good if cut into strips and used on edge.

It is best to avoid glass, since most types are not very hard and shatter easily. However, large glass marbles, if well embedded, can be a useful alternative for eyes. With care, coloured glass 'smalti', made for use in vitreous mosaics, can also be used for small details.

These suggestions are but a few. In any locality, special products can be found; provided that the material is *hard* and non-porous, it *can* be used. But exercise restraint: too many artificial colours and textures will make your mosaic appear garish.

Looking for pebbles

Finding good pebbles is half the battle! There is no short cut. Some garden and landscape suppliers may offer them for sale, but sources are very limited and bulk purchases are seldom suitable. For work of high quality, you will usually have to collect the stones yourself. Beaches, rivers and quarries are the main hunting grounds.

However, you cannot search wherever you like, or take just any pebbles you find. The legal situation may differ from country to country, or even from state to state, but the foreshore where pebbles are found usually belongs to somebody, whether a person, a company, a local authority or the State. To keep within the law, you must find out who the owner is and get permission for access and permission to remove stones.

It would be most unusual for anyone to object to an amateur mosaicist hand-picking stones and carrying away a bucketful or two. However, the taking of

Stone-picking on a bank of shingle at a local river.

'threshold stone' gives a personal stamp to any patch of ground. The sea-captain might have an anchor on his doorstep, like a badge of office. A family might make a visual pun on their name (a Fox, a Castle, a Mill). Trade emblems can be used; traditional heraldic devices; star signs; or, equally, one could choose 'the picture I would most like to see when I open my door to the world'.

In the garden the scope is endless: a favourite seat or arbour; the spot where one always pauses to contemplate the view; the passage from public to private; the familiar site for afternoon tea; all these can be stamped with completely idiosyncratic choices which have meaning to the persons involved and give an identity to the place for others.

Designing a small piece of pebble mosaic works in the same way as a little picture: you put it in the right place where it complements its surroundings, and 'frame' it with slabs, flags or bricks.

Large civic designs

On a civic scale, an area may have historical associations with a particular character or event. Emblems may be drawn from heraldry, maritime insignia,

Contrasting pebbles make a simple but very effective zig-zag pavement in Rhodes.

architectural detail and fanciful logos. A more spiritual approach might generate images of unity, freedom or peace.

In large public areas, pebble mosaics can be extremely effective. They can point up features and delineate sidewalks, breaking up large and daunting areas of paving. Above all, they can act as textural elements within the larger scheme, visually drawing together the different surfaces. Ideally, they should be an integral part of the design, rather than a pebble picture filling a hole in the pavement; a brief encounter in a sea of concrete flags.

Disciplines of groundscape design

Our visual perception of the groundscape beneath our feet varies according to our viewpoint. Looking down on a mosaic from a window or a high terrace, you will be able to see a large design or pattern laid out across a square. However, when you are on the same level as the mosaic, looking down, you can only focus on a small area immediately around you; and, as you look forward across the space, the perspective viewpoint radically changes the appearance of the design.

There is no point in designing an elaborate image which can be appreciated only from an aeroplane. Even where there is a higher vantage point, a mosaic should be conceived to satisfy the viewer at ground level. In a large design this can be achieved by making a succession of individual images within the overall design. The challenge to the designer is to make perambulation over the area a satisfying experience, so that the viewer is drawn from one place to the next.

The direction of this movement relates to the positioning of architectural features: the entrance, the middle, the corners or intervening areas, the edges, the exits. Because the eye takes in only about 2m (6ft) ahead at any one moment, appreciation of the general layout is very limited.

Positioning designs

Designs which have a definite top and bottom can be frustrating when viewed the wrong way up. They should ideally be used only in a position where there is one main approach or viewing point. However, including images which face in other directions, perhaps in a border, makes them easier to accept. Design motifs which twist and turn, displaying something interesting in all their different aspects, no matter from which direction they are approached, are particularly useful.

The discipline of floorscape design is, of course, as

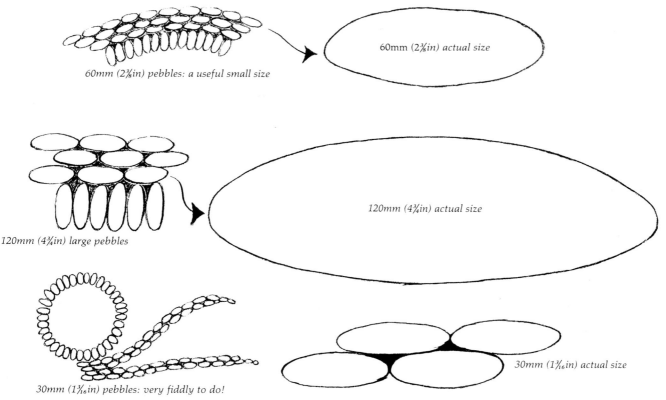

Pebble sizes drawn to scale 1:10 and actual size.

60mm (2⅜in) pebbles: a useful small size

60mm (2⅜in) actual size

120mm (4¾in) large pebbles

120mm (4¾in) actual size

30mm (1³⁄₁₆in) pebbles: very fiddly to do!

30mm (1³⁄₁₆in) actual size

old as the concept of the decorated floor itself. Historical sources, which document the design solutions that different cultures have generated, deserve some study. Although very little information is available dealing specifically with pebble floors, illustrations of traditional mosaics, tiled floors, oriental carpets and many other forms of design from around the world will provide inspiration. Bookshelves are full of good design ideas for those who bother to look.

Working with pebbles

Having covered the general principles of suitability and orientation, let us return to the pebbles themselves. It is always a good idea to go back to the beach to pebble-hunt and to play! Surrounded by infinite materials, you can get to know the many patterns and textures to be made with different kinds of pebbles. Browse through all the shapes and sizes and colours, experimenting and combining. This way you will learn the basic vocabulary of a craft which has a language all its own. I recommend playing before you do any drawing.

Clarity and contrast

It is not always easy to obtain pebbles of good contrasting colours, and it makes sense to use what is easily available in each locality. Therefore, it becomes

even more important to achieve a design which is clear and bold, and not to attempt anything with too much detail.

The clear silhouette of an heraldic lion is enlivened by placing the pebbles for the mane in a zig-zag pattern, by a realistic 'eye' stone, and by ferocious teeth carved from hard white marble. The background of white limestone pebbles gives a good contrast to the main figure.

31

Basic weave with longs. Offset the pebbles in the row, and keep the width of each line constant — 'fat' rows and 'thin' rows.

A good effect is made by gradually reducing the size of the pebbles in the rows.

LONGS
Skimmers are the most expressive pebbles. They give flow and direction to the design.

Do the outer rows first, then the centre. Then work out the remaining rows and pick the pebbles to fit.

Lines need at least two rows of stones.

CYLINDERS
These make an attractive all-over texture. A range of different sizes is needed in order to fit them together without gaps. Pick the size to fit the space.

When graded for size, cylinders make many attractive patterns.

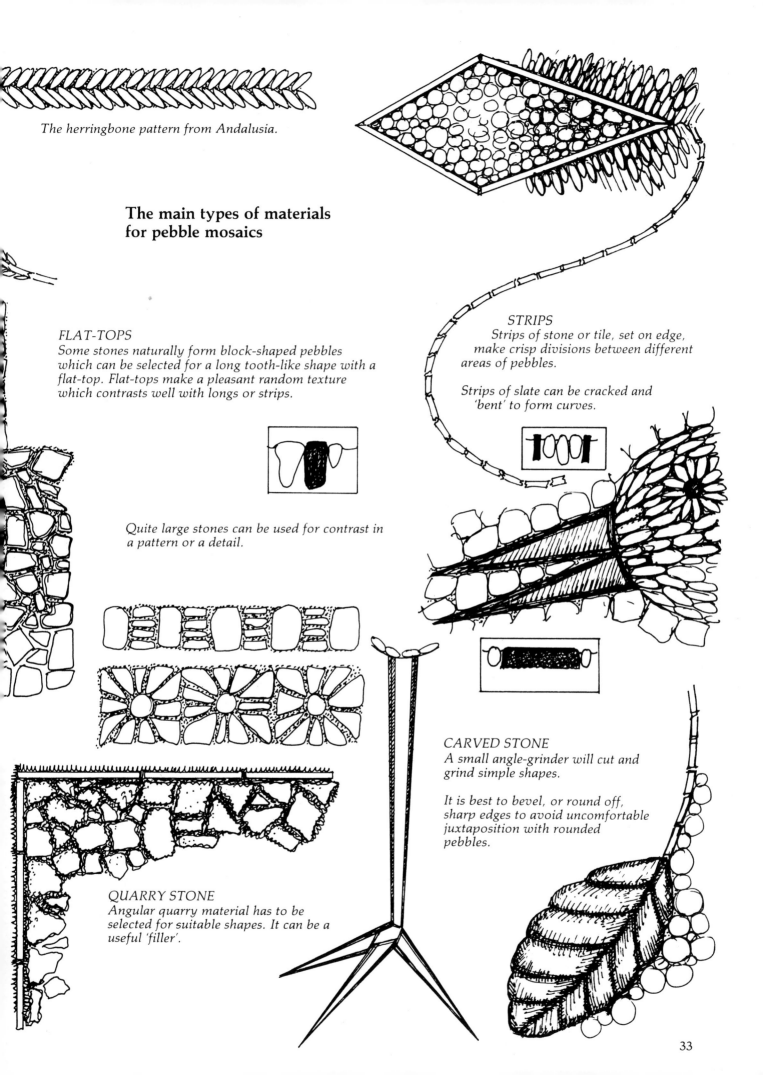

The herringbone pattern from Andalusia.

The main types of materials for pebble mosaics

FLAT-TOPS
Some stones naturally form block-shaped pebbles which can be selected for a long tooth-like shape with a flat-top. Flat-tops make a pleasant random texture which contrasts well with longs or strips.

Quite large stones can be used for contrast in a pattern or a detail.

STRIPS
Strips of stone or tile, set on edge, make crisp divisions between different areas of pebbles.

Strips of slate can be cracked and 'bent' to form curves.

CARVED STONE
A small angle-grinder will cut and grind simple shapes.

It is best to bevel, or round off, sharp edges to avoid uncomfortable juxtaposition with rounded pebbles.

QUARRY STONE
Angular quarry material has to be selected for suitable shapes. It can be a useful 'filler'.

33

Making a design

A typical starting point is a small sketch: the back-of-the-envelope type of doodle which nonetheless carries conviction. You need to plan out what sort of pebbles to use, and how to interpret the design with the different shapes; possibly adapting one to the other.

Those who lack ideas or drawing skills may find it easier to work from something they have seen and adapt it for their purposes. A photocopier is a valuable tool for exploring design ideas, allowing motifs to be copied and cut up so that experiments can be

An attractive feature of Italian pebblework is the placing of pebbles to follow particular directions, as in this leaf. It is particularly effective over a large surface, where the angle of the sun in the evening dramatically highlights the effect.

One big stone of the right shape (it must be a flat-top) says everything; much better than a lot of small pebbles.

Stones placed like this will emphasize a detail.

Placing the background pebbles in an opposing direction to the flow of the motif will help definition.

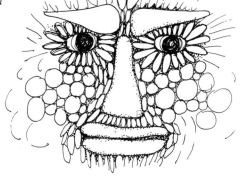

Clarity and contrast

The best contrast will be obtained by simple bold outlines. The way in which pebbles are arranged within an area will add interest.

Use the flattest side on the edge of an area

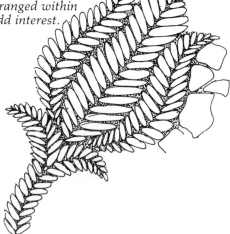

An example of a border using stones of a similar tone and colour. Contrast is achieved through size and shape alone.

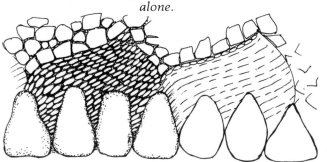

34

made with different arrangements, borders and backgrounds.

Using paper cut-outs

You may recall, as a child, cutting out snowflake designs from folded paper, where the cut-out shapes reproduce symmetrically along the folds in a most satisfying and effective manner! This schoolroom occupation can still be a useful trick for quickly generating a host of geometric patterns or repeating motifs, or simply to make multiples of a motif from several sheets of paper, using the repeats to play around with different arrangements.

When experimenting in this way, it is a good idea to use black or dark paper which will give an instant impression of the two-dimensional effect. Having found a rough idea that pleases you, you can go on to make more refined versions through careful drawing and cutting.

Blocking in a line drawing

Other designs will probably begin as a line drawing, but it is hard to visualise the finished effect from this alone. Shading in areas will show the effect of the contrast between the different coloured pebbles, and help you to see whether the composition is balanced and satisfying. Ask yourself the following questions:

- is the silhouette of the motif satisfying in itself?
- does it 'read' as leaf or flower or hand?
- are the lines (if any) decisive and clear and wide enough to be made in at least two lines of pebbles?
- do the black and white shapes have a decorative value apart from their subject-matter?

Be critical! Adjusting a design is the work of minutes, or perhaps a few hours. The labour of making the mosaic is a hundredfold; and living with it, a lifetime.

A useful trick is to cut out a design in black paper. Cutting out prevents too much detail being included and enhances the two-dimensional quality.

Colouring in a line drawing to be solid black and white will show up weak points and help to balance the composition.

Treading warily

A word of caution. Certain themes and subject matter, when applied to stone pavements, can affect people in an unfortunate way. They can be afraid to tread on particularly emotive images ('Why should beautiful white birds be trodden underfoot?') Some reactions to human imagery in stone can be equally disturbing, especially in a lonely setting and in an unfamiliar medium. Perhaps it is because the more the human figure is expressively distorted, the more disturbing it becomes. Whatever the reasons, these things should be considered, although it would be a pity to make hard-and-fast rules to restrict a designer's freedom.

Let the stones speak

There is a fine line to be drawn between perceiving an arrangement of stones as a mundane collection of pebbles and making an imaginative leap that simultaneously perceives them as an image. It is part of the fascination of pebble mosaic that a few stones can be so well chosen and placed that this transformation is achieved.

A final few words of advice on design: search for stones; feel their particularity, the effects they make when you play with them; look out for the shapes which suggest the curve of an ear, or a sharp claw. Try using one stone instead of a dozen to stand for a nose or a jewel. Let the stones suggest to you the form they would like to take.

One of the easiest design effects — laying long pebbles in different directions — has been exploited to the full in this geometric design by Rafael Gimenez in El Brillante, Cordoba. Long evening shadows emphasize the design and add an almost three-dimensional quality.

SCALE DRAWINGS

Advice for beginners

Making a scale drawing is useful for any project larger than the doorstep cameo. The scale of 1:10 (1cm on plan = 10cm in reality) is the easiest and most useful scale for pebble mosaic projects up to 5m (16ft 3in) across, as it is possible to draw the actual size of pebbles to scale. Therefore, you can check that the design will be effective, and that it is practical to do it! It is easy to get carried away with a pencil and to put in more detail than it is physically possible to accomplish with pebbles.

A modern photocopier which enlarges and reduces in one per cent stages can be very useful when an existing drawing needs to be converted to a different size. Get the machine operator to programme it to convert the size of the drawing to the desired measurement for a scale drawing. It is easy to adapt the blown-up photocopy to your purposes; cut it up, play about with it, and eventually make a fair copy on tracing paper.

To draw to scale you will need paper, ruler, compasses, protractor, set square, pencils, etc. Graph paper can be used if it gives you confidence, but it is not necessary. However, you will have to remember those school geometry lessons — keep a sharp pencil and measure accurately.

When drawing to scale, metric measurement will be found much easier to use than feet and inches. If site measurements have been taken in feet and inches, it is worth while, before starting, converting them to metric scale using a tape marked with both metric and imperial measurements. For the scale 1:20 (1cm on plan = 20cm actual size) and other metric scales, a scale ruler is useful, with the conversion already marked on the ruler.

If you prefer to work in feet and inches, make sure that the ruler is marked with appropriate subdivisions (twelfths, eighths, etc.) and whatever you do, do not mix metric and imperial scales (e.g. 1cm = 1 foot). The arithmetic gets crazy!

Metric scales

1:10 is the most useful scale for pebblework projects up to 5m.
1:20 for larger projects over 5m.
1:5 for small projects under 2m.

Imperial scales

1 inch = 1 foot (1:12)
1 inch = 8 inches (1:8)
1 inch = 2 feet (1:24)

Note: When drawing to scale, it is helpful to get an idea of the size of the pebbles you are intending to use. (See diagrams on page 31.)

A complete example of making a scale drawing from a thumbnail sketch and translating the design into pebbles is included in the step-by-step examples on pages 48–53.

Drawing to full size

When a template or stencil is required, only part of the design need be drafted up to full size; but the procedure is the same as for the whole design.

To enlarge a design, impose a grid of lines at regular intervals on to the scale drawing. I use lines at 50mm intervals representing 500mm on the scale 1:10; but if you find these squares too large, try 25mm (representing 250mm). A similar grid of lines is drawn on large sheets of paper or board at 500mm or 250mm intervals. Then, taking each square one at a time, transfer the information to the larger size. Concentrate on the main lines of the drawing. You can take a critical look at the overall design once it is sketched in actual size, and then adjust the details.

Blowing up large designs

The following only applies to the drafting of very accurate full-size cartoon drawings for pre-cast technique.

It requires some preparation and special equipment to maintain accuracy on large drawings. First, the workplace needs to have a dry, smooth floor large enough to accommodate the full-sized design.

White cartridge is the most suitable paper to use: it will not stretch or distort, provided that it is kept dry. It can be obtained in continuous rolls up to 3m (10ft) wide from specialist suppliers (commercial photographers use it as studio background material).

As an alternative to drawing on paper, white-faced hardboard in large 2.4 x 1.2m (8 x 4ft) sheets can be taped together to form a continuous surface. A jigsaw with a fine blade will be needed to cut out the desired shapes. This method is particularly suitable for pre-cast techniques where the thickness of hardboard serves as a useful base for each mould.

Some large-scale drawing equipment can be improvised. A long straight-edge can be made from a length of timber 100 x 20mm (4 x ¾in). Check for straightness by eyeing down its length, and correct with a plane if necessary. (Long metal straight-edge rulers can be bought from builders' merchants, but are expensive.) Fine string will be needed for the longest lines, stretched taut between drawing pins (thumb tacks). The line can then be marked along its length, and the marks joined with a straight-edge. For measuring, use a steel tape which does not stretch over a distance.

A long compass can be made quite simply by· punching holes into lengths of old steel tape and inserting a drawing pin (thumb tack) into one end, and a pencil point into the other. To get a true right angle, my usual method is to use intersecting arcs of equal length from both ends of the first base line, joined to its centre. Or you can use Pythagoras: mark 3m (10ft) along a base line; use the 'compass' to draw an arc 4m (13ft) from that point, and another of 5m (16ft 3in) from the other end. Join the point where the arcs intersect to the ends of the line and you have a true right-angled triangle.

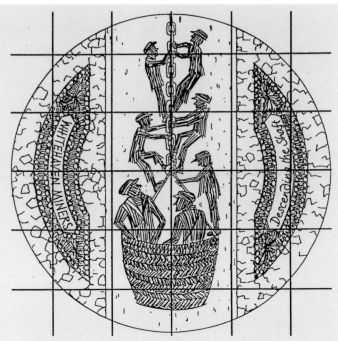

On the scale drawing of this design (reduced here) grid lines were drawn at 50mm intervals to represent 500mm actual size.

Using the line and compass is the most accurate method of setting out a large design. It is easy to subdivide angles to 45° and to make 60° angles by recalling your school geometry lesson. Once you have established the main lines accurately, subdivisions can be made by measuring with the steel rule and drawing along a straight-edge.

Making an actual-size cartoon. The author blowing up a design commemorating the mining community of Whitehaven. The design is transferred by enlarging from the small squares on the scale drawing to the large squares on the paper. Because this design is being made by the pre-cast method described later, the drawing has been reversed to a mirror-image.

Equipment needed: a long straight-edge, a 'compass' made out of a length of old steel tape and a drawing pin (thumb tack), and a steel tape for measuring. A cardboard cutout of a section of the chain helps with the drawing of repeats. It is useful to check the sizes of pebbles to be used against the drawing. In this example, the figures needed adjusting to ensure that small pebbles could be fitted neatly into corners.

MAKING PEBBLE MOSAICS IN SITU

Preparation and planning

Turning your design into a mosaic still requires some thought. The ground must be prepared to receive it and guides for the design marked out. Check that you have all the necessary tools and constructional materials, and sort pebbles into accessible piles or containers.

When planning the physical construction of the mosaic you must allow for drainage. Wherever possible, the finished pebble mosaic surface should be kept just above the level of the adjacent ground so that it will always be well drained and clean. In addition, a 'fall' must be established: the surface must be slightly tilted so that rain runs off. Mosaics on flat sites will have to be 'crowned'. Nothing spoils a mosaic more than puddles which leave a film of dirt, algae and finally moss.

A straight-edge and spirit level can be used to establish a level over short distances up to 3m (10ft). Hammer wooden pegs into the ground at convenient points on the perimeter of the mosaic, and use the straight-edge on top to check when they are level.

To establish a level over a large area, use a builder's level or a water level. A water level can be made from a length of transparent polythene or PVC tubing full of water, but make sure there are no trapped air bubbles. Fix one end to a stake and extend the pipe across the area (topping up with water if necessary). The level of the water at both ends will always remain the same. This level can then be marked on pegs set into the ground, enabling you to measure down the pegs and mark the necessary fall.

On a flat site, a 'crown' will be desirable: the perimeter pegs are set level with each other, and the

central peg is set higher. On a large mosaic, intermediate pegs will be needed and these should be placed in convenient locations for setting up formwork, to be used as described later.

The base

The reason why many old cobbled areas are now uneven is because their bases were not made to withstand heavy lorries and farm tractors; all that was required of them was that they should be strong enough to bear the weight of people and horses. Demands upon working surfaces today are much greater, but if the underlying base is strong enough to withstand the weights to which it will be subjected, the mosaic will be perfectly durable.

The edges

In addition to having a strong base, it is important to prevent damage to the edges of a mosaic. Strong support may already exist in the form of a house wall or a kerbstone (be careful to keep the pebble surface 150mm (6in) below any damp-proof course in a house wall). If no support exists, it will be necessary to construct a good edging with setts, stone slabs, bricks or concrete products. Again, the strength of its construction must correspond to the traffic which the mosaic will have to bear.

Mosaic for pedestrian use

All the soft topsoil must be removed, and the site excavated to the level of the subsoil. The amount of excavation will vary according to the site; however, at least 200mm (8in) is necessary to accommodate a minimum base layer of 100mm (4in) rammed hard-

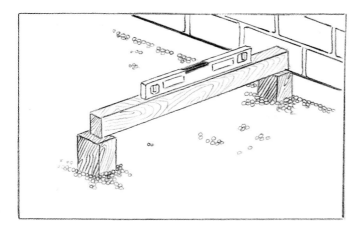 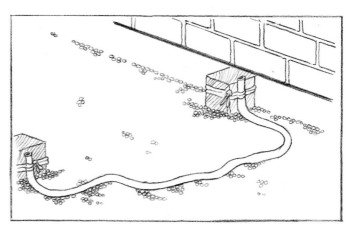

Levelling with a straight-edge (left) *and levelling with a hosepipe* (right). *The water level will be the same at both ends of the hose. Mark the levels on the pegs and measure down on the peg to establish the fall.*

core beneath the pebble working depth of 100mm (4in), and it will probably be necessary to excavate deeper. It is important to get down to hard, undisturbed subsoil, without organic matter. If clay is encountered, which might be subject to 'frost heave', it should be removed to whatever depth is recommended by local practice.

Scrap brick and stone must be rammed down with sufficient gritty sand to fill the gaps and bring it to a level. If purchasing stone for the base, try to obtain granular material of size 40mm (1½in) down to dust. If the excavation is deep, a layer of larger rocks in the bottom is advisable. It is most important that the base material is thoroughly compacted. If possible, a small vibrator or 'whacker' should be hired to ensure thorough compaction.

The edge restraint should be set on a foundation of 1:2:4 concrete (1 part cement to 2 parts concreting sand to 4 parts 10–14mm (⅜–⅝in) aggregate), 100–150mm (4–6in) deep, and haunched up at the sides as shown on the profile drawing.

The depth for the pebble layer is determined by the depth of the largest pebbles to be used. A working depth of 100mm (4in) will be found adequate for large pebbles, whereas 50mm (2in) will be plenty for finer work.

Over the consolidated hardcore, the pebbles are set into a filler layer of sand, or sand and cement, as described below.

Pebble mosaic for driveways — light vehicle use

Preparation of the site is broadly similar to that for pedestrian use, except that a greater depth must be excavated. In addition to the minimum base layer of 150mm (6in), it may be desirable to incorporate a 100mm (4in) layer of concrete for additional strength. Edge restraint and haunching should be substantial.

Pebble mosaic for heavy vehicle use

The loads of heavy vehicles pose a particular problem which has to be tackled site by site, in consultation with the road engineer responsible for each project. However, pebble mosaic made by the pre-cast method has proved satisfactory in a narrow street in Edinburgh where delivery vehicles frequently turn. It was specifically designed for this situation, with adequate foundations and edge restraint (see page 58).

Profile of a pebble mosaic laid for pedestrian use only.

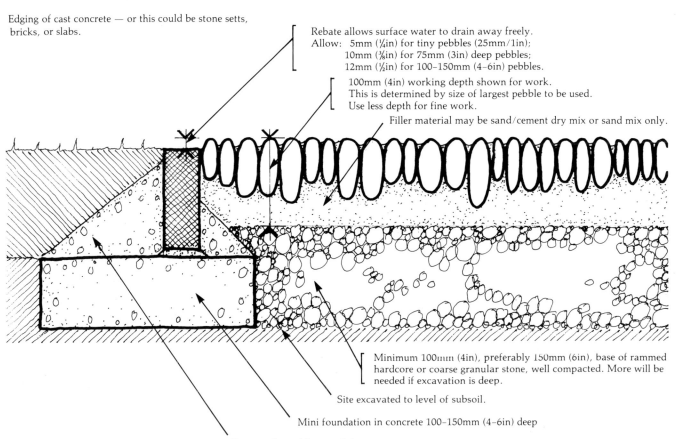

Edging of cast concrete — or this could be stone setts, bricks, or slabs.

Rebate allows surface water to drain away freely.
Allow: 5mm (¼in) for tiny pebbles (25mm/1in);
10mm (⅜in) for 75mm (3in) deep pebbles;
12mm (½in) for 100–150mm (4–6in) pebbles.

100mm (4in) working depth shown for work.
This is determined by size of largest pebble to be used.
Use less depth for fine work.

Filler material may be sand/cement dry mix or sand mix only.

Minimum 100mm (4in), preferably 150mm (6in), base of rammed hardcore or coarse granular stone, well compacted. More will be needed if excavation is deep.

Site excavated to level of subsoil.

Mini foundation in concrete 100–150mm (4–6in) deep

Concrete haunching to edging

A robust treatment makes an attractive feature of this courtyard.

Right This alley in Carmona, a small village in Spain, has been divided into manageable sections with double lines of thin bricks laid on edge. The lines follow the fall required for effective drainage, and the miniature brick 'walls' act as guides for tamping down the intermediate sections of pebblework. It is a pity that the workmen lingered so long at their siesta that they failed to scrub down the mortar grouting applied to the left-hand section!

Profile of a pebble mosaic for a driveway or light vehicle use.

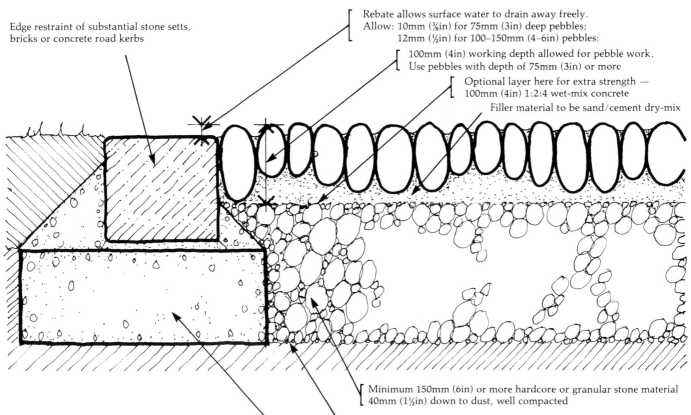

Edge restraint of substantial stone setts, bricks or concrete road kerbs

Rebate allows surface water to drain away freely.
Allow: 10mm (⅜in) for 75mm (3in) deep pebbles;
12mm (½in) for 100–150mm (4–6in) pebbles;

100mm (4in) working depth allowed for pebble work.
Use pebbles with depth of 75mm (3in) or more

Optional layer here for extra strength —
100mm (4in) 1:2:4 wet-mix concrete

Filler material to be sand/cement dry-mix

Minimum 150mm (6in) or more hardcore or granular stone material
40mm (1½in) down to dust, well compacted

Site excavated to level of sub-soil

Concrete foundation, well haunched on outer edge

Getting started: subdividing the area

A system of subdividing the internal area must be made in order to facilitate the laying of pebbles and tamping them down to the correct surface level. This applies to all mosaics measuring more than 1m (3ft) across.

For plain cobbling of large areas, the most practical subdivisions are made permanently, before pebble-work begins. Bricks, setts or bands of stone slab can be laid in lines, on mortar, often contributing effectively to the overall pattern. They will govern the fall of the entire finished surface.

Another method is to construct bands of pebble-work at regular intervals using a sand/cement mix. They must be allowed to set firmly enough to form tamping guides for the intermediate pebblework.

A more intricate method can be borrowed from Chinese pavements, where strips of slate or shards of roof tile are set out in a regular geometric pattern prior to pebblework. A complete latticework of miniature walls is constructed to the correct surface level, using stretched strings as guides for both the fall and the intersecting grid of the pattern.

Temporary subdivisions are used when the pebbles cover the whole surface. Wooden formwork made from lengths of timber 50 x 100mm (2 x 4in) is held firm by pegs driven into the base. Lengths of steel rod about 12mm (½in) (or very stout tent stakes) are ideal — they will withstand repeated hammering and are more easily forced into the hardcore base.

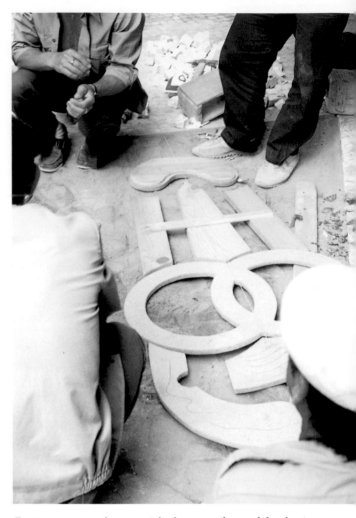

Portuguese workmen with the stencils used for laying a repeat pattern.

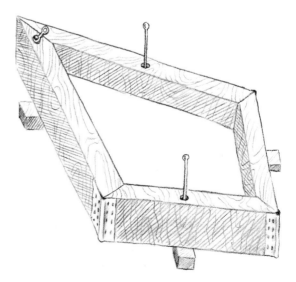

A wooden stencil, for the repeated oak-leaf design shown, is split into two halves, joined by hooks and eyes.

A stencil, which also serves as the formwork for the diamonds in the mosaic around a garden table (described on pages 48–53), is made of timbers joined with leather hinges so that it can be easily removed.

For a repeating design, it will be helpful to set formwork in parallel bands of matching width, or, for a circular pattern, radiating from the centre. With free-form designs, you may prefer only to erect those necessary for current work so that they do not encumber your working space; but with a freehand 'a mano' approach over a large area, it will still be necessary to mark the key points of the design with pegs.

Templates and stencils

Where a design uses repeated motifs, cut a template out of plywood (chipboard or hardboard are both cheaper and may be adequate for small numbers of repeats). This can be placed in position on site as a guide to shape and size. Use the scale drawing to accurately scale up the motif on the board and cut it out using a jigsaw fitted with a fine blade.

A template is useful for the placing of formwork and temporary supports for pebbles. Even more useful in practice, if you have many repeats to do, is to make a stencil by constructing a surround to the templates. Thick plywood should be used, reinforced with extra wood around the perimeter as necessary. This can be placed in the correct position for the pebblework, held in place temporarily with pegs, and wedged up to the correct level. Stencils are more convenient to use when split into two halves and fitted with hook fasteners, so that they can be removed easily when the pebbles are in position.

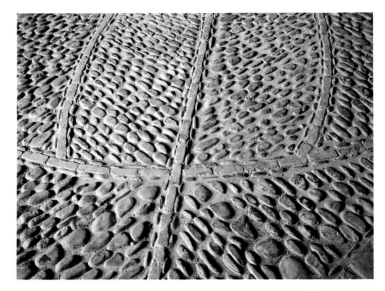

The ancient carriage road leading to the Alcazar Palace in Seville. The lines of large stones divide the road into geometric segments and establish the levels of the crowned surface.

Placing the pebbles

The pebbles are bedded into a layer of sand, or sand and cement mix, spread over the consolidated hard-core. Many old cobble pavements were laid in sand alone, and perfectly sound pebble mosaics can be made like this today. However, it is important for either filler that the sand should contain a mixture of particles, so that it will pack down solidly when

The sun mosaic on page 2 being made by the author.

water is applied. An angular gritty structure is best. For most work, the particles should be from 5mm (¼in) down to dust. For fine work with tiny pebbles, use 3mm (⅛in) to dust.

As each section of the mosaic is completed, the pebbles are tamped down and the filler consolidated by thorough wetting as described in the following chapters. Finally, sand is brushed between the pebbles to produce a final level, leaving a suitable 'rebate'.

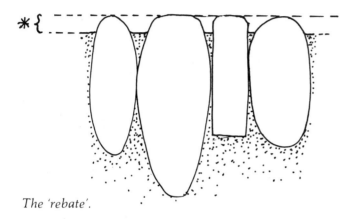

The 'rebate'.

Wet-mix concrete

This technique, using wet concrete instead of a dry sand and cement filler, is suitable only for plain work, using larger-scale pebbles. The work has to be done quickly, within the setting time of the concrete.

Subdivide the area into sections suitable to use up one mix at a time. Take care to keep the surface of the pebbles clean, and keep them close together. Allowing them to spread out loses strength, and looks terrible!

The whole operating procedure of wet-mix pebble-work requires good organization and a bit of practice to get it right. You need to spread more or less the right amount of mix so that, as you press in, pack in and then tamp down the pebbles, the mix rises up between them, *but not over them*. A few test areas will help to establish the optimum quantity to use in relation to the types of pebbles.

The 'rebate'

I have borrowed the word 'rebate' as it is the nearest description I can find for an important physical detail of pebble mosaic. The rebate is the distance that the pebbles protrude above the finished surface of the filler material. Because pebbles are worn and rounded, the more you level off the surface with filler, the less you see of the shape of the pebbles.

Filler mixes: advantages and disadvantages

Sand alone
3 parts 5mm (¼in) grit
2 parts sharp sand
1 part building sand

- is cheap and pleasant to use.
- allows some natural drainage through the pavement: useful around trees. Drainage also helps to maintain the tightly packed composition of the mix.
- allows more leisurely laying.
- allows greater freedom in design approach. A large area can be worked in 'a mano' technique.

But
- you must find suitable sands or mix your own.
- it will eventually grow weeds so must be watered with weed killer and occasionally cleaned with a scraper.
- frost may lift pebbles and crumble the surface.

Dry sand/cement mix
Designed to resemble a concrete mix on a miniature scale.
3 parts 5mm (¼in) grit
1 part sharp sand
1 part building sand
1 part cement

- weedproof if used with a sand and cement finishing mix (provided that débris of leaves, etc. is brushed away occasionally).
- allows lots of time to work on details.
- should not be affected by frost.

But
- cement costs more.
- hands need protection.
- no drainage through pavement so a proper fall over the surface is essential so rainwater can drain away.
- a suitable mix of sand and grit has to be found.

Wet-mix concrete
3 parts 10mm (or ⅜in) aggregate
2 parts concreting sand
1 part cement
Add an air-entraining plasticizer to increase workability, and a retarder to give longer working time, in accordance with the manufacturer's instructions.

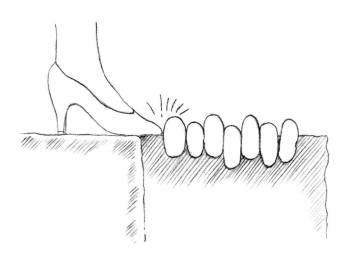
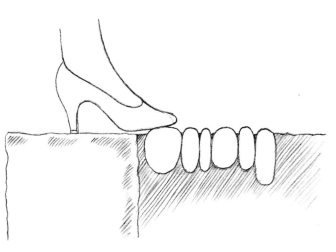

The edges of a pebble mosaic need attention.

Make sure that rainwater can drain off freely and will not be trapped into pockets by any slate or other linear materials you may use.

Suggested levels for rebate are:
12mm (½in) on larger sizes of pebble (75–100mm/3–4in)
8mm (⅜in) average size pebbles (50mm/2in)
6mm (¼in) on fine work (25mm/1in)

Although maintaining a suitable rebate is essential to the finished appearance of the mosaic, it can cause a problem at the edges of the work. Use larger rounded stones to make a comfortably graded rise in level at these points.

Good working practices
- keep the sand covered (it is difficult to make a semi-dry mix if the sand is sopping wet).
- keep the stones clean (the cement bonding is spoiled if the stones are dirty with soil).
- if the stones are from a beach, wash them (salt is bad for concrete).
- only mix enough for each day's work. Even dry mix will harden up overnight and be full of lumps.
- protect hands. Prolonged contact with cement will cause dryness, irritation, even dermatitis. Use gloves or barrier cream.
- get as comfortable as you can on the ground. Those who kneel should protect themselves with knee pads. Various small stools or boxes will help to alleviate the inevitable strain of working on the ground.

A pavement in the Cemitario do Alto de S João, Lisbon, Portugal. The use of wooden stencils aids the execution of these crisp designs. First one colour is placed, then the stencil is removed and the other colour is filled in. Notice the individual shaping of the blocks to fit the design. When working with pebbles, individual stones with a straight side can be selected to achieve such clear lines, or other materials, such as strips of slate, can be incorporated.

TWO STEP-BY-STEP EXAMPLES

This section shows each stage in the making of two *in situ* pebble mosaics: the first, a modest threshold stone; and the second, a rather more complicated geometrical design. Both are intended to explain the processes of construction more thoroughly.

1. Two little fish

This is the sort of project which a beginner could attempt. The mosaic marks the entrance to a fish-pond area of the garden where a path passes through an opening in a clipped box hedge; a modest site, but one where a little incident is welcome.

A thumbnail sketch is all that is required for this size and location — 800 x 500mm (32 x 20in). The design is simple: two little fish with a herringbone border.

To begin with, the full width of the path is dug out down to the subsoil, leaving plenty of room to set up the edging. Slabs of sandstone (quarry offcuts) are used here, 150mm (6in) deep, bedded on a mix of concrete which is haunched both sides, particularly on the outside. Gaps of 5mm (¼in) are left at the corners to allow for drainage.

The base is made of clean scrap stone and sand, and pounded till it is absolutely solid. Its level is made 50mm (2in) below the surface of the path, because the pebbles to be used are quite small, varying from 30 to 50mm (1 to 2in) deep. The space is then half filled — 25mm (1in) — with dry-mix sand/cement. Since the pebbles are small, a finer sand is preferable. This is trodden down firmly and its surface flattened using a block of wood.

Next, using the freehand 'a mano' method, the design is drawn into the mix with a finger or a stick. Do not worry if you get it wrong: just 'rub it out' and try again.

Now the pebble laying can commence. The pebbles are pressed into the mix so they are held up by it and stand vertically. In this example, the border

Below *Pebbles gradually build up the fish shape as they are pressed into the filler mix, following hand-drawn lines.*

Right *The 'a mano' mosaic is completed with a final spray after sand has been brushed between the pebbles to leave a rebate of about 5mm (¼in).*

47

The first rough sketch for a design to go around

Blocking in the design in black and white makes the effect clear.

is made first, then the fish motif, and finally the background is filled in. The top edges of the pebbles are allowed to stand above the level of the edging by about 5mm (¼in). This edging will be the finished level, so the pebbles are tamped down to it, using a length of timber. As such small pebbles are used this operation is gentle.

On completion, the mosaic is soaked with water from a fine spray. When the pebbles have dried, a final top-dressing of sand/cement mix is brushed in with a paintbrush, leaving a 5mm (¼in) rebate between the top of the pebbles and the sand/cement surface. A sheet of polythene protects the mosaic as it cures.

2. Dining al fresco
This is a more ambitious project than the two little fish and calls for more preparation and patience. The mosaic was designed as the surround for an outdoor pedestal dining table, already set up in a favourite spot in my garden. Its size was decided on site by measuring the distance needed for the garden seats to rest comfortably upon it, and allowing plenty of space for pulling back and for relaxing after large alfresco dinners!

The design
A simple sketch was the beginning of this project. I wanted a radiating design to emphasize the round table, but one simple enough for ease of execution. I chose black and white stones, and this suggested a band of same-sized black 'longs' around each diamond, which would be made from white flat-tops. The idea was adjusted on the scale drawing to accommodate these bands, and I went stone collecting, knowing the size of pebbles I needed.

Site information	Measurements for 1:10 scale plan
Diameter of mosaic = 290cm (114in)	29cm (11.4in)
Radius = 145cm (57in)	14.5cm (5.7in)
Diameter of central post = 56cm (22in)	5.6cm (2.2in)
Radius = 28cm (11in)	2.8cm (1.1in)
Edging of setts (average size) = 12cm (5in)	1.2cm (0.5in)
Number of diamonds = 12	

Note: Metric measurements are easier to convert to various scales, and particularly to my favoured scale of 1:10. However, measurements taken in inches can be converted using a ruler marked in tenths of an inch.

Using ruler and compass, I drew the circles for the outside perimeter of the mosaic, the central post and the sett edging, using the measurements converted to 1:10 scale. A protractor was needed for dividing the circle into twelve segments. I experimented with different types of diamond shapes: some touching each other, some regular, some touching the central post. I decided on a regular edging of black pebbles to the diamonds and the perimeter border, and adjusted the shapes of the diamonds to fit. Colouring in the shapes of the diamonds gave a much better idea of the effect the mosaic would have.

A scale drawing 1:10
(reproduced actual size).

74 cm

34 cm

97 cm

Scale 1:10

It is well worth spending time and trouble at this stage. Little alterations can easily be made on the plan and may make a great deal of difference to the finished effect.

Having drafted out the design, it was a simple matter to put a ruler on the plan to measure the irregular shapes and convert back to actual-size measurements, multiplying by 10. In this design, it was important to know the measurements of the diamond shape so that I could make a template. I also needed to know the distance between the points of the diamonds to place the template accurately on site for the construction of each diamond.

Measurements to use on site
Internal length of diamond = 970mm (38in)
Internal width of diamond = 340mm (13½in)
Distance between radiating lines at perimeter = 740mm (29in)

Excavating the site
All the soft topsoil is removed until the hard undisturbed subsoil is reached. Often this means a spade depth of 300mm (12in), sometimes more.

Hardcore
Hardcore of clean scrap brick and stone is rammed down with sufficient gritty sand to fill the gaps and well compacted to 100mm (4in) below the level intended for the finished mosaic surface.

The edging
The edging of black granite setts is set on a mini-foundation of 100mm (4in) of concrete. This provides an adequate perimeter to protect the edge of the mosaic.

Setting out the fall
With a long length of timber and a spirit level, 'key stones' are set to mark the high and low points of the 'fall', with enough intermediate stones to keep it consistent over the whole surface. Then it is a straight-

1 *Excavating the site.*
2 *Filling the excavation with hardcore.*
3 *Ramming the hardcore level.*
4 *Setting out the fall with a spirit level.*
5 *Dividing up the circle.*
6 *Placing wooden battens as formwork.*
7 *Positioning the stencil.*
8 *Placing the pebbles.*

1

2

5

6

forward job to complete the circle of setts, working from one 'key stone' to the next.

The sett edging and a marked line around the central post act as guides for setting up formwork for the pebbles.

Setting out the pattern

The perimeter is marked off at twelve points, using the measurement derived from the scale drawing, i.e. 740mm (29in). Pegs are hammered in at these points and strings attached to divide the circle into twelve segments. The pedestal of the table is already a permanent fixture. Not being able to move it adds a slight complication and calls for improvisation. Without it, only one central peg would be required.

I made a plywood template of the diamond shapes, taking measurements from the scale drawing.

Placing formwork for the pebble mosaic

100 x 50mm (4 x 2in) formwork of timber is a suitable size: substantial enough to withstand the force of ramming down the tightly packed pebbles, and deep enough to take up most of the depth. This is placed in position and wedged up to the correct level with pieces of slate or roof tile. About 12mm (½in) is added for the rebate.

Pegs made from 300mm (12in) lengths of steel rod are hammered down into the base to stop the timber moving out of position.

Note: In general, formwork placed to subdivide the area into sections of about one square metre or a square yard will be found convenient.

Here is a method of delineating the motifs. Using the diamond template as a guide, 100mm (4in) deep strips of ply or chipboard are propped up to make the shapes. The area is half filled with a sand/cement mix and trodden down firmly. These temporary walls help to keep the edges straight and the shape correct. Having filled the diamond with pebbles, the strips are gently removed, and the rest of the area can be filled in.

4

8

Placing the pebbles

The area between formwork is half filled with sand or sand/cement mix and trodden down firmly. A certain amount of loose mix must be kept on hand to work around the pebbles as the operation proceeds.

Pebbles are pushed down into the mix until they stand slightly above the formwork level.

A rounded stick (the wooden end of a mallet/hammer handle serves) is used continually to firm the mix *underneath* each pebble. The same tool doubles as a sort of scraper to push up the loose mix as required. Keeping the mix firmed underneath the pebbles ensures that there are no pockets of loose stuff, which would later sink and form a weak spot

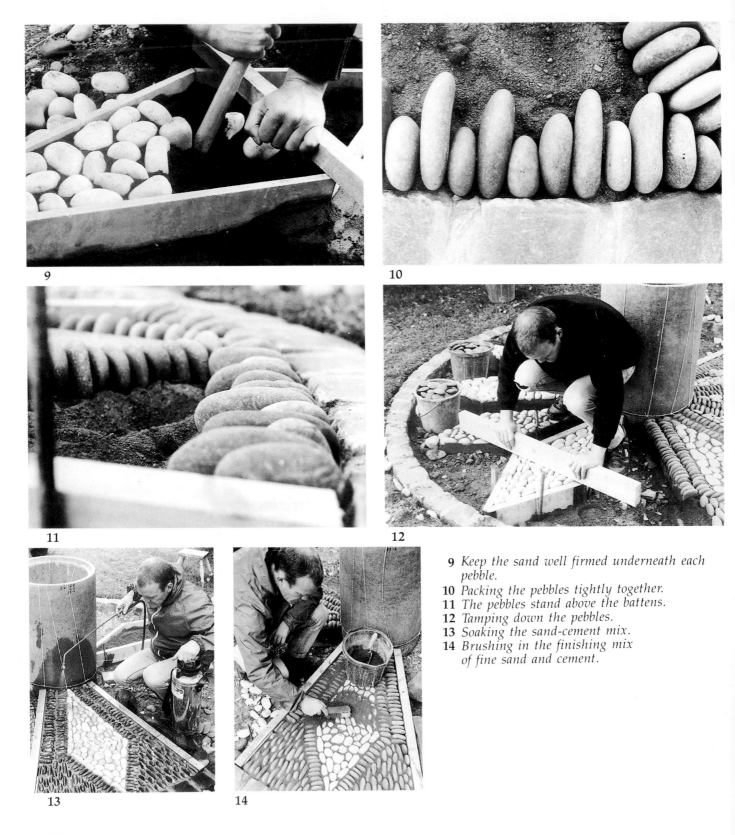

9

10

11

12

9 *Keep the sand well firmed underneath each pebble.*
10 *Packing the pebbles tightly together.*
11 *The pebbles stand above the battens.*
12 *Tamping down the pebbles.*
13 *Soaking the sand-cement mix.*
14 *Brushing in the finishing mix of fine sand and cement.*

13

14

The completed mosaic makes an attractive addition to the garden.

for the entry of water and the formation of ice particles in freezing weather.

It is important to pack the pebbles closely together. They should be touching each other in the vertical plane, without gaps. This is the strength of the construction — all the pebbles are so tightly wedged together and interdependent that there is simply nowhere for them to go. Leaving gaps introduces the possibility of a sideways movement — and should one pebble ever escape the ranks of its neighbours, a landslide could occur. The pebbles would fall like a pack of cards, resulting in a pothole in the pavement.

The pebbles are now standing about 12mm (½in) above the level of the formwork.

Tamping down the pebbles

Vigorous action with a strong straight piece of wood is called for until this tamping bar rests level on the formwork. As the pebbles are forced *down*, they displace some of the underneath mix which is forced *upwards* between the pebbles.

Finishing off

The base sand/cement mix must now be thoroughly soaked with water to consolidate the mix around the pebbles as well as activating the cement. Leave overnight (or until convenient to complete the mosaic), and keep completely covered by a polythene sheet to prevent drying out.

To complete the final surface, the polythene is removed to allow the pebbles to dry off. A top mix of fine (mortar) sand and cement, mixed 3:1, is brushed over the surface until a satisfactory effect is achieved. Then water is gently sprayed on with a garden-type pressure sprayer until the mix is thoroughly soaked. If any little holes appear, the operation is repeated.

After being left covered for three to four weeks to cure, the mosaic is finished.

A PRE-CAST TECHNIQUE FOR PEBBLE MOSAIC

The main problem in making *in situ* pebble mosaic is the weather. It is a time-consuming occupation, and there is a limit to how long one can work exposed to cold wind or baking sun. Rain makes it impossible to proceed. It is a task for perfect days when the child-like pleasure of playing with pebbles and sand is increased by the anticipation of a useful and beautiful end result.

Climate considerations apart, kneeling or crouching for hours on end is a deterrent, especially for those who are not young. The pre-cast method, which I have devised, bypasses these problems. The work can be carried out in the comparative comfort of a workshop, at a bench height convenient for sitting or standing.

The mosaic is divided into manageable pieces, which are later assembled on site like a jigsaw puzzle. The pieces are made separately, and construction follows the principle of the 'upside-down cake' — first put in the plums, then the syrup, lastly the cake mixture; when cooked, turn over.

It may sound easy, but I am afraid it is not. Achieving good results requires a great deal of application and practice. Those who are new to pebble mosaic should wait for some good weather, and start with several *in situ* pieces, to get experience in selecting and placing pebbles.

Reversing the image

The design for the mosaic is drawn up full size as described on pages 37–38. Since the pre-cast method is a reverse technique, it is essential that the actual-size cartoon drawing is also reversed (unless the design is symmetrical). If not, when the cast slabs of the pebble mosaic are turned out, the design will be the wrong way round.

The easiest way to reverse the image is to make the scale drawing on tracing paper, and make a reverse print on a photocopier. This is then used for drafting up the actual-size drawing.

The mould is set up on or around the base pattern.

To divide up the mosaic into manageable segments, the joints are drawn in with a thick marker pen, 10mm (⅜in) wide. It is best to draw the joints where they least disturb the flow of the design, or where they form a latticed background, like the leadwork in stained glass. Half a square metre (about 5 sq ft) is the maximum area for each segment. The larger it is, the heavier it gets.

The cartoon is now cut up along the centre of the marked joints, and all the pieces numbered on a scaled plan to avoid confusion later. These numbers will be scribed on to the back of each slab as it is cast.

Constructing the moulds

Each segment requires an individual mould. For repeats, a wooden or fibreglass mould can be constructed.

Each piece of the pattern is placed on to a strong flat board and an individual mould is constructed around it. The depth of the mould depends on the size of the pebbles, but 75–85mm (3–3½in) is both convenient and strong. The sides of the mould are built up from lengths of timber, blocks with curved edges, sections of PVC pipes in varying curves, and any other materials which match parts of the profile.

The walls of the mould are held together with strong adhesive tape, and kept in position by blocks of wood nailed into the baseboard. The whole construction is temporary, but has to be firm enough to withstand tamping and vibration at the casting stage. Accuracy is important: the walls of the mould must be true 90°, and the precise perimeter edge of the pattern must be followed — or else the pieces of the jigsaw will not fit!

Placing the pebbles

The pebbles go in with their intended top surface placed downwards. They are packed vertically together in exactly the same iceberg fashion as for *in situ* work. It is necessary to visualise the right side up first, and then deliberately place the pebble face down.

At the same time as the pebbles are put in, dry sand is worked around them in the bottom of the mould to provide the rebate — sand which is later

Right *A wooden mould is used here for repeated sections of a circular border. Sealed with varnish and waxed before each use, such a mould can be used twenty or thirty times. More use than this would require a specially made fibreglass mould. Here extra sand is being added to even up the sand layer.*

Pebbles are placed upside down into a layer of sand in the bottom of the mould and sand is worked around them.

washed away (average 10mm/⅜in). It is very difficult to imagine what is going on underneath irregularly shaped pebbles, and to achieve a consistent depth of sand requires practice. Any little mistake can spoil the finished effect. Use a thin stick with a notch to test the depth and fill up thin patches by dribbling in more dry sand. A small paintbrush is useful for working the dry sand around the pebbles as the work proceeds.

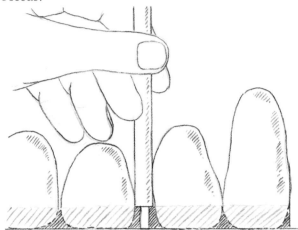

Testing the sand depth with a notched stick.

Pouring in the grout

A layer of grout is needed to fill up the gaps between the pebbles and to penetrate the tiny crevices between them down to the sand layer. A non-shrink cementitious grout should be used to eliminate the shrinkage problem of ordinary cement mortars. It is produced as a ready-to-use blend of Portland cements, fillers and additives. Various brands are available from larger builders' merchants.

Before pouring the grout, soak the sand by spraying with water from a fine pressure sprayer. The grout is mixed with water, according to the maker's instructions, and poured all over the pebbles. A gentle hammering on the table all around the mould helps release any trapped air bubbles. Allowing a couple of hours for the grout to set partially to the firmness of fresh putty will prevent pebbles being disturbed during the concreting stage.

Filling the mould

A mix of concrete is prepared — 10mm (⅜in) aggregate, concreting sand, and cement in the ratio 3:2:1, using the minimum possible water to attain a workable consistency. A concrete plasticizer is a useful addition. The concrete is packed into the mould, tamped down, and (if possible) gently vibrated on a vibrating table at the lowest setting. The slab should be covered with polythene overnight, to prevent loss of moisture.

Turning out the slabs

The slabs can be turned out the following day, except in cold weather, when it is safer to leave them for two days. In fact, they are not literally 'turned out', but the mould materials are stripped away, the slab

Grout is poured over the pebbles, filling all the spaces between them.

The mould is filled with concrete, which is then tamped down and vibrated.

turned over and the sand hosed off. The slab should be treated carefully as it takes at least three days to achieve strength, and it will become even stronger throughout the curing period of four weeks.

Any little blemishes can be rectified at this stage. If, for example, grout has seeped through on to the surface of the pebbles it can be chiselled off, and any small air holes can be filled with tiny dabs of fresh grout.

Curing

Each slab needs to cure for four weeks, and should be enclosed in polythene during this period to prevent water evaporation.

Installation

A properly made cast slab, after the full curing period, is very strong indeed. But care should be taken when packing them for transportation: *slabs should be stacked on edge* and firmly wedged to prevent damage to the corners.

The installation procedure is similar to that used for laying any large-scale concrete slabs, except that the extra depth of mosaic slabs, and the various shapes, make the job more challenging. It should be remembered that concrete in slab form is strong in *compression* but not in *tension*: such a force could break it.

Bedding the slabs

Site preparation should broadly follow the directions given in the chapter on *in situ* mosaics. Each slab is bedded on approximately 25mm (1in) of mortar (3:1 sand and cement), using a mix which is slack enough

Putting in the last slabs of a pebble mosaic garden feature. Finished mosaic on front cover.

Ring of radial-shaped paving blocks — e.g. 'Keykerb'.

Sand and cement mix joint.

Pre-cast cobblestone rose motif 88mm (3½in) deep.

Sand and cement bedding 50mm (2in) deep

2,000mm (6'8")

Concrete, class 30/20, base 200mm (8in) thick, with steel reinforcement fabric, B785, 1700mm (68in) diam, with minimum 50mm (2in) concrete cover to steel.

Class 1 mortar.
Concrete class E foundation and haunch.

Paving bricks 80mm (3in) deep.

Sand bedding 50mm (2in) deep.

Road base 100mm (4in) deep.

Sub-base, type 1, 150mm (6in) deep.

Cross-section of road and mosaic at Rose Street, Edinburgh, showing the reinforced base and heavy edge restraint which were used in this application.

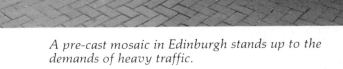

A pre-cast mosaic in Edinburgh stands up to the demands of heavy traffic.

to enable the slabs to be knocked down with a rubber mallet to exactly the right level. Make sure there are no stones underneath the slabs as this could cause cracking when under the weight of a vehicle.

Fitting awkwardly shaped pieces of the jigsaw puzzle, especially the last piece, requires the use of strong straps (climbing tape, old seat belts or plastic banding tape) to lower them into position. When they are level and properly bedded, the straps can be withdrawn.

Grouting the joints

Finally, the joints between the slabs are filled, using more non-shrink grout, which is carefully poured from a jug. Then all that is needed is a final wipe over to remove spills, and covering over with protective polythene sheeting for a few days to protect the mosaic.

DESIGN IDEAS

A pebble mosaic is made up of tiny patches of colour, like the brushmarks of a pointillist painting or the stitches of embroidery. Each stone in a pebble mosaic represents one mark or dot, and to make a recognizable shape a considerable number of such marks are needed. It follows, therefore, that in a small mosaic, such as a threshold stone, the imagery should be simple with a clear outline and a minimum of detail. It should be able to be 'read' without difficulty by everyone who sees it.

In larger mosaics, it is possible to attempt a more complex drawing of images and to explore details of tone, pattern and decoration within the motif. However, motifs should still be kept simple and bold, especially when augmented with geometrical borders, scrolls and similar connecting devices.

Unfortunately, machinery and mechanical subjects, whilst they may be representative of industry and trades, are difficult to translate into the medium of pebbles. Pebble mosaic is intrinsically more suited to organic subjects and the natural world. Although the history of a place may present an overwhelming case for including a subject such as a beam engine in a pavement, efforts to bend the medium to the purpose are likely to be disappointing. Direct carving or sandblasting the imagery on stone is a better solution because the precise detailing of the subject can be reproduced.

A pattern from the Alhambra, Granada, Spain.

Patterns based on grids with circles and arcs.

From Guimaraes, Portugal.

From the Generalife, Granada, Spain.

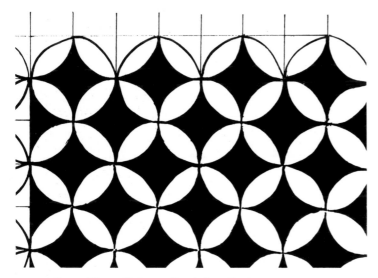

From Viana Palace, Cordoba, Spain.

All-over patterns

Repeated patterns give a wonderfully rich, carpet-like effect to larger spaces. Borders help to tie the lively surface to the topography of the site. The larger the area, the more they repeat and the more impressive they become.

The examples here are drawn from Spain, Italy, Portugal and Madeira. Some are very simple and all are effective. Simple stencils would be necessary for the construction process.

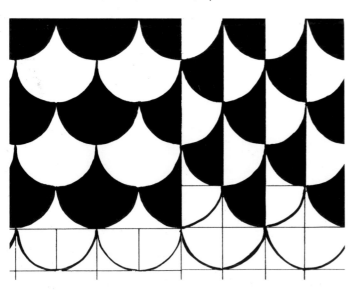

A shell pattern from Madeira and a variation of it from Guimaraes.

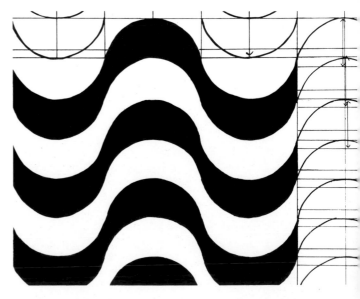

Traditional Portuguese sea pattern used in the Rossio, Lisbon, and in Rio de Janeiro, Brazil.

Three colours are used in a carpet pattern at the Villa Medici, Fiesole. Note the border pattern.

Right The sophisticated treatment of a pavement in Seville is based on a squared grid and shapes which interlock in an irregular pattern. Borders are left as plain bands.

Below A simple repeat pattern on steps in Lisbon's Botanical Garden radiates from the centre and continues, one row at a time, down the steps.

An optical effect produced by dividing hexagons into diamonds in three colour tones. All verticals and diagonals are parallel. From Elvas, Portugal.

Above right *An interlacing pattern based on square grids, superimposed at 45°. From the Alhambra, Granada, Spain.*

Below *Traditional Chinese patterns from* Yuan Ye (The Craft of Gardens) *by Ji Cheng, first published in 1631. Slate or stone could be used to divide the straight-edged patterns. (See also the photograph on page 11.)*

Pebbles combined with other materials

Many attractive patterns can be seen in Spain, where pebbles are used as a textural 'filler' with arrangements of slabs, setts, bricks or tiles. These other materials serve two practical purposes: they reinforce surfaces which must bear the extra weight of vehicles, and they establish falls over the entire area.

Pebbles combined with local marble; the chequered design set diagonally in a street in Ronda, Spain.

Light grey limestone pebbles as an infill with bricks and glazed ceramic tiles at the Alhambra, Granada.

Lines of stone paving blocks divide a Granada street into squares of approximately 600mm (2ft). These are quartered by thin bricks or tiles on edge, and then filled alternately with black or white pebbles.

Bricks, laid on edge in a traditional Islamic pattern based on superimposed squares, form a frame for pebbles. Some of the bricks are carefully cut to fit. From a courtyard in Seville.

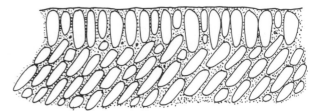

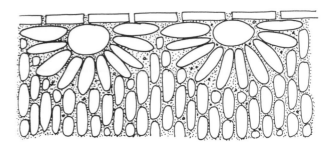

The simplest types of borders for small mosaics.

Borders

On the smallest and simplest scale, a border such as a single row of long pebbles with each one pointing towards the centre has a pleasing effect.

Large decorative borders are beautiful in themselves; they also emphasize and contain motifs, enhance areas of plain pebblework, and help to relate the pebble mosaic to the architecture and topography of a space. Twists, meanders and plaits are easy patterns for borders, which can be adapted to different stones and colours.

A 'twisted ribbon' design from Braga, Portugal, which could be interpreted in pebbles.

Below *An exquisite scroll pattern from a terrace of the Villa Garzoni. The shape is emphasised by a row of white 'longs' outlining the black scroll. The border is set off by a contrasting edge of red pebbles. A form or template would be used to maintain the regular shape of the scrolls.*

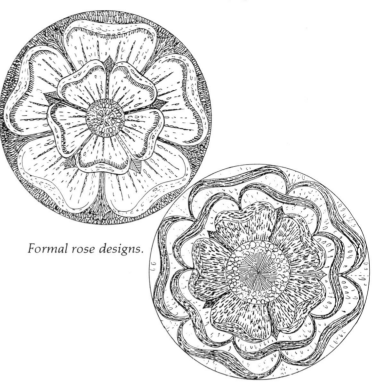

Left *An heraldic rose adapted to a large formal design. Sprays of rose leaves in slate make a surface contrast with the rest of the pebble surface. Another aspect of this commemorative mosaic is seen on page 28.*

Formal rose designs.

Flowers and leaves

Flowers can be presented in profile, 'flat on', or as fully opened blossoms seen from above. Botanical accuracy is impossible. Leaves, fronds, tendrils and stems are useful in all kinds of arrangements, both for their own decorative value and as connecting links curving through a design.

Below *Flowers made from riven slate fragments with bright quartz pebble centres. These were pre-cast in moulds 300mm (1ft) across and later incorporated into a large area of plain* in-situ *pebblework.*

Set into stone flags, this 1.8m (6ft) mosaic incorporates a ring of points for stars and a red moon in each corner. Seen from the balcony behind, it presents a smiling face.

Left *Design for a 16-ray sun with a wave border, suitable for a fairly large mosaic, about 3m (10ft) in diameter.*

Below *This moon shape is outlined by the surrounding crazy paving. The simple changes to the basic shape — an eye, a nose, a line for a mouth — make a character.*

Sun, moon and stars

A sun can be a complex design with many wavy arms and points or the simple spiky shape a child might draw. Is there a man in the moon? Has the sun a face? What is certain is that celestial images are easily identifiable and successful pebble mosaic subjects.

Basic star shapes can be given an almost infinite number of variations: four, five, six or more points; thin or thick and with various middles. Like the sun, a star is very suitable as a motif for a circular centrepiece.

A lucky find of wedge-shaped slate offcuts led to this sun mosaic, cast in four slabs, each 600mm (2ft) wide.

A cheerful doorstep design using spiky slate offcuts, with flints for the eyes and pieces of floor tiles for the mouth. The background of flat-top white limestone has the simplest of borders — large stones pointing inwards.

A star form in a garden patio. Only 1m (39in) across, its small area is accentuated by encircling rows of setts.

An expansive treatment of a moon, asleep and sprouting flowers and sparks like dreams, designed by the author for a pool 4m (14ft) across.

Below Tiny stars cut from hard Portuguese marble contrast sharply with an overall texture of flat-tops.

The finished mosaic of the sleeping moon at the Stoke-on-Trent Garden Festival. The colours of pebbles are brilliant when seen under water.

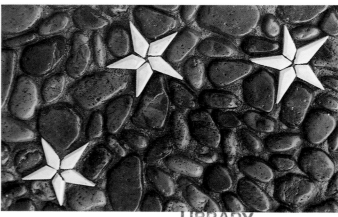

Pebbles are graded for tone to accentuate the contours of this puffing face, representing a wind.

Right A mosaic by the author adapting a Celtic interlacing design to make a comment on the relationship of human beings to Nature.

Human figures and animals

Little 'stick' figures, like those children draw, are easy to make in strips of slate or tile. With the use of a little imagination, they can be very expressive and work well against a contrasting background. Clothed figures can be a problem, and the details of twentieth-century dress can be frustrating. Unless clothing is formal or decorative, it is easier to forget it altogether and adopt a style of asexual nudity, or merely to suggest clothing in the overall silhouette of the figures.

Slate is a marvellous material for making long spiky shapes, suggestive of the angular wings of many birds, and of the swiftness of flight. Such angular pieces are found when slate is obtained as offcuts or scrap, with the grain lying vertically to the surface.

Small pieces can be riven with a cold chisel and hammer applied along the grain (use goggles to protect your eyes from flying splinters). Slate can also be

A mosaic in Whitehaven, north-west England, incorporates a lettered scroll and carved bas-relief mermaid, both cut out of slab. The mermaid's body is mainly flat, with lines cut to a maximum depth of 20mm (⅞in) with an angle-grinder. The scales on her tail are typical of the curved grooves which are easy to make with this tool. The lettering has been hand-carved with tungsten-tipped chisels.

A pebble mosaic figure of a medieval knight. Black 'long' pebbles in rows suggest chainmail, while the sword has been cut from a single piece of slate, strongly bevelled. Note how single stones are used to suggest the details of elbow-guards and a jewelled sword belt.

Slate fragments are invaluable for human figures. This mosaic was made for a playground for handicapped children.

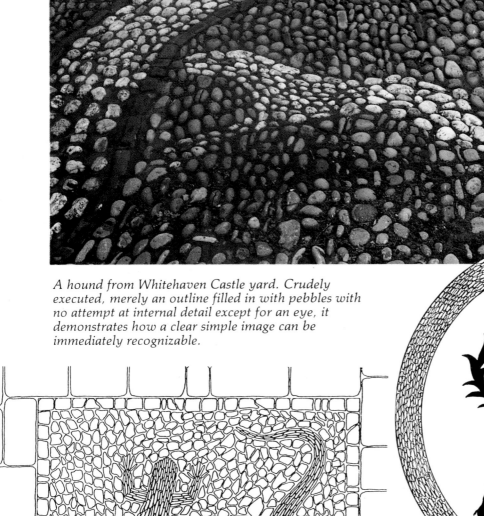

A hound from Whitehaven Castle yard. Crudely executed, merely an outline filled in with pebbles with no attempt at internal detail except for an eye, it demonstrates how a clear simple image can be immediately recognizable.

A design for a barking dog intended to be 2m (6½ft) across.

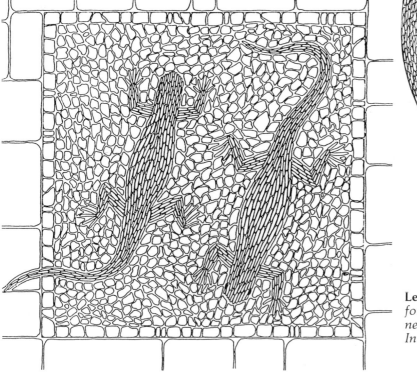

Left A newt design by Mark Currie, 2m (6½ft) square, for a rural patio. A nice touch is the way in which the newt's tail is carried over into the surrounding paving. Intended to be made in longs and contrasting flat-tops.

A modern example of pebble mosaic on the Greek island of Rhodes.

cracked and 'bent' to form curved lines. In this case, strips of around 12mm (½in) width are laid with the grain parallel to the ground for cracking. Strips up to 25mm (1in) wide can be used, but it is more difficult. The cracked pieces are reassembled with the grain vertical, to make lines in the mosaic. All riving of slate entails a lot of waste, even with plenty of practice.

A mosaic at Keighley, Yorkshire, incorporates the town's motto and interweaves its heraldic emblems: water, snake, and dragon.

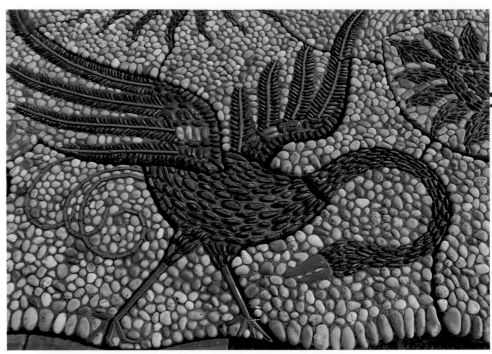

Long black pebbles, carefully graded for size, suggest feathers, with cracked and bent green slate midrib. Carved green slate legs and beak and a black marble eye give additional interest. However, the main effect rests upon the decorative shape of the bird contrasting with the light background of rounded 'cylinders'.

Left *Irregular riven fragments of slate are used for the swallow in this 600mm (2ft) diameter piece, contrasting with a background of rounded flints.*

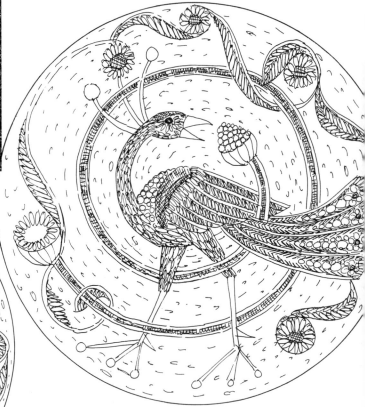

Decorative bird designs by the author, suitable for mosaics about 2m (7ft) in diameter.

A mosaic 750mm (30in) wide, based on the small dolphin in the accompanying design. This one was simplified in the making, as pebble mosaics often are. It is always difficult to make the stones fit the drawing but, as long as you start off with a clear bold idea, the results are usually recognizable.

This fish's fluted fins and tail are carved from limestone slabs. Such oddments can often be obtained from monumental masons. Obtain hard stone to match the durability of the pebbles. An impression of scales is given by selecting rounded stones for the main body and a glass marble makes a good eye. 'Cracked-and-bent' slate is used in the border. The round stones on the head are a man-made material called Regulox, used in industrial grinding of pigments for paints and glazes. Note how the contrast is made between the fish, which is all light-coloured stones, and the background of long dark pebbles — a contrast in both tone and shape of pebbles.

A dolphin design suggested by the discovery of long sensuously-shaped stones in a river which flows through a glacial deposit.

Right A bold dolphin design from Portugal.

This ship has been drastically simplified and stylized to adapt the design for pebblework, and the rigging had to be reduced to a minimum. The sun's rays and the breath of the wind-face give an interesting movement to the background pebbles.

Ships and the sea

Maritime imagery has many attractive motifs for pebble mosaics. Take your pick from all kinds of boats and sailing ships, waves, Neptune, mermaids and mermen, ropes, anchors, shells, octopi, starfish, and all kinds of fish.

Ship designs intended for mosaics 2.5 and 3m (8 and 10ft) wide.

An anchor-and-rope design for a mosaic about 2.5m (8ft) wide. The hatching on the anchor and rope indicates the lie of the pebbles.

This elegant little ship is a lovely design from Lisbon.

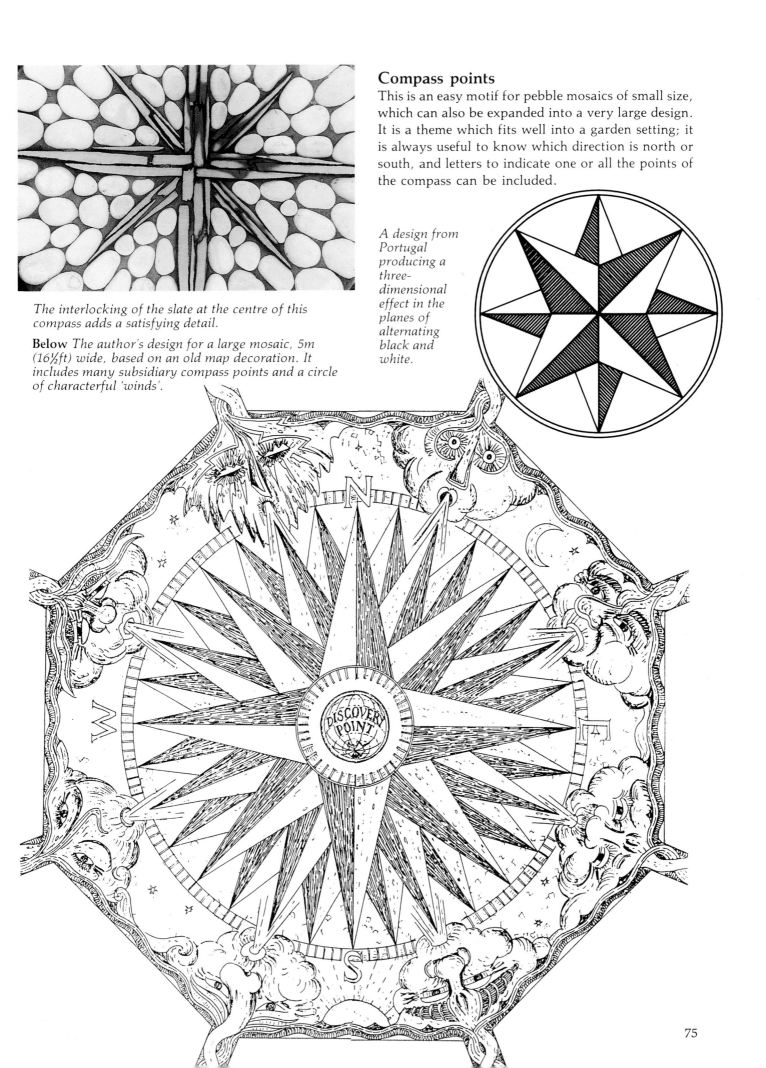

The interlocking of the slate at the centre of this compass adds a satisfying detail.

Compass points

This is an easy motif for pebble mosaics of small size, which can also be expanded into a very large design. It is a theme which fits well into a garden setting; it is always useful to know which direction is north or south, and letters to indicate one or all the points of the compass can be included.

A design from Portugal producing a three-dimensional effect in the planes of alternating black and white.

Below *The author's design for a large mosaic, 5m (16½ft) wide, based on an old map decoration. It includes many subsidiary compass points and a circle of characterful 'winds'.*

DISCOVERY POINT

This small mosaic 1600 x 800mm (63 x 31in), made for a school for partially sighted children, provides a variety of tactile experiences, as well as an interesting pattern.

Left *A design for a large-scale mosaic made principally from graded flints. In this case, good quarry material (usually sold for drainage) was available in a range of sizes. By hand-sorting the stones, and laying them in lines of diminishing width, it is possible to create attractive fan-shaped patterns.*

The author's design for a traditional 'running' maze in which, rather than getting lost, the participant follows the whole pattern to reach the centre. The design provides amusement, especially for children, as well as making an attractive motif.

Knots and mazes

Both Celtic and Islamic sources are rich in knotwork patterns with their effective interlacing. The many different kinds of mazes and labyrinths are also useful subjects for pebblework.

Only two examples can be shown here, but there are many sourcebooks which can be consulted. Look for simple ones: however gorgeous the examples you find, most will be too complicated to make unless the work is on a very large scale.

Commemorative mosaics

The qualities of permanence and durability make pebble mosaics an appropriate medium for commemorating births and special events, or for memorials. In the public sphere, civic and historical events are obvious opportunities for figurative pebblework which might be located in community gardens, or gardens of remembrance.

In the making of a pebble mosaic, all kinds of stones can be incorporated, and many people can participate in collecting the pebbles. I was recently commissioned to make a 'birthstone' for a child. Family, godparents and friends were all asked to bring a special pebble to the christening, and these were then arranged to form a design based on the Tree of Life. The exercise of choosing which pebble to bring gave added interest for the guests and an extra activity to the christening party, and the result has an enduring significance for the child as he grows up.

A simple mosaic for a family grave. Commissioned as an alternative to the standard covering of marble chippings, the pebble mosaic will keep its decorative appearance when relatives are unable to give the grave regular attention. Family members each brought a choice of pebble — a varied and marvellous collection — all of which were incorporated into the design.

A birthstone for a child. Pebbles contributed by friends and family form the fruits on the Tree of Life. A background of gravel contrasts with the motif in this small mosaic, only 600mm (2ft) square.

Mosaics by children

Most children feel the fascination of pebbles, and delight in mixing and making concrete pies. However, the technical demands of making durable pebble mosaics are difficult for youngsters to grasp, and it can be disappointing if the results turn out badly. Although pebbles are difficult to manipulate correctly, children can use other materials with more immediate satisfaction. Small pre-cast mosaics can be made with readily available disposable moulds, such as tomato boxes with solid hardboard bottoms. Children collect their own pebbles, and these are augmented with cracked tiles and plates, coloured glass smalti and different coloured gravels. Pictures can be made either by pressing the elements *into* wet concrete in the mould, or by placing into sand in the bottom of the mould and then filling with concrete. Either method requires considerable adult supervision to ensure the children handle the concrete safely, and to help them to achieve a satisfactory result. Their efforts can be very charming and reasonably long-lasting.

'Tomato-box' mosaics made by children at Flimby School, Cumbria. They incorporate coloured tile, small bright coloured smalti and gravels, which are easier for children to manipulate than pebbles.

Lettering and numbers

Dates and house numbers, inscriptions and mottoes, can all be made in pebble mosaic. Lettering needs to be simple and open in form, and executed in pebbles which contrast sharply with their background. Long pebbles laid across the width of the letter are effective, as seen in the Spanish greeting shown here.

A gateway greeting by Raphael Gimenez in Cordoba, Spain.

A letter carved from slate slab and inserted into a pebble mosaic.

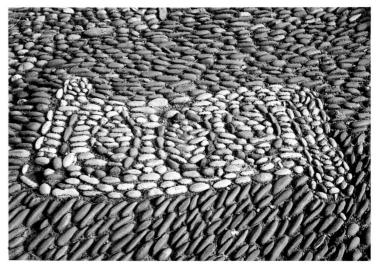

A date in vernacular style at Lytham St Annes, England.

In Portugal, precise Roman numerals are made using a stencil.

Classic lettering from the Villa Garzoni, Italy, shows the precision achieved by a careful choice of pebbles.

INDEX
Figures in *italics* refer to illustrations